The 5-Minute BIBLE STUDY for Women

Print ISBN 979-8-89151-140-8

Published by Barbour Publishing, Inc., 1810 Barbour Drive, Uhrichsville, Ohio 44683, www.barbourbooks.com

Our mission is to inspire the world with the life-changing message of the Bible.

Printed in the United States of America.

Valorie Quesenberry

The 5-Minute BIBLE STUDY for Women

Seeking God's Heart

INTRODUCTION

Do you find it hard to make time for Bible study?

You intend to, but inevitably the unexpected happens or you hit the snooze button one too many times; then the hours turn into days, and soon, another week has passed and you have not picked up God's Word.

Don't despair! You CAN do this.

This book provides an avenue for you to open the Bible regularly and dig in to a passage—even if you have only five minutes! That's right. Five minutes used well can be life changing when you spend them with the Savior. Think about Zacchaeus in the tree or the woman at the well!

Here's a plan for how to use this book:

- **Minutes 1–2:** Read carefully the scripture passage for each day's Bible study.
- **Minute 3:** Understand. Ponder a couple of prompts designed to help you apply the verses from the Bible to your own life. Consider these throughout your day as well.
- **Minute 4:** Apply. Read the devotion based on the day's scriptural focus.

- **Minute 5:** Pray. A prayer starter will help you to begin a time of conversation with God. Remember to allow time for Him to speak into your life as well.

I hope *The 5-Minute Bible Study for Women* will help you establish the discipline of studying God's Word. One of the best ways I have found to make time for an important daily task is to plan it around things you already do. If you drive to work, why not head out to your vehicle five minutes early with this book and your Bible? If you're a stay-at-home mom or you work from home, why not plan time while your children eat breakfast or during your morning coffee break to delve into this doable Bible study? Your willingness to spend these minutes focused on God's Word and prayer can make a huge difference in your day!

FINDING GOD

READ JEREMIAH 29:10–14

Key Verse:

"You will seek me and find me,
when you seek me with all your heart."
JEREMIAH 29:13 ESV

Understand:

- What childhood memories do you have of playing hide-and-seek?
- How does God promise that seeking Him will be different than looking for hidden friends?

Apply:

A lifetime of playing hide-and-seek sounds exhausting. But, thankfully, God has completely different rules than we did as children. He wants to be found by us.

He delights in being found by us. Our peers may have prided themselves on staying hidden the longest. Not so with the God of the universe. He has been waiting for us to find Him since we first got lost in the garden long ago through the sins of our ancestors, Adam and Eve. He came looking for them while they cowered from Him, ashamed and guilty. And He promised to send a Savior to bring all humankind back into relationship with Him. If we let Him forgive and restore us, we can spend the rest of our lives seeking Him through a friendship that gets better every day. This kind of seeking isn't the difficult kind, but the rewarding and fulfilling sort of "work" one puts into a relationship.

He commits to giving us more than we could have dreamed. He promises that we will find Him and His abundant life.

Pray:

O God, how often I forget that You want me to find You! You want to meet me in the morning before my day begins, and You want to talk to me in the evening about what happened in those hours of daily life. Though I have been found by You in salvation, I always want to remember that seeking You every day gives me more joy and security than any other thing I can do. Thank You for rewarding me with Your presence. Amen.

KNOWING GOD'S HEART

READ 1 PETER 1:13–21

Key Verse:

Since it is written,
"You shall be holy, for I am holy."
1 PETER 1:16 ESV

Understand:

- What does the description of God as "holy" tell us about His heart,
- the core of His being?
- What security does this bring to us as we seek to know Him better?

Apply:

We have been lied to by Satan. He tells us that the holiness of God is a reason we should run from Him. But, actually, the opposite is true. The reason we can run toward God and be assured of His love and mercy and faithfulness is His holiness. Because He is the essence of holiness, He is never deceptive or hypocritical or capricious or unreliable. Because He is absolutely holy, He is perfect love and perfect goodness and has perfect plans for us. We can be utterly confident that He will always work for our highest good, even in the things we don't understand. We can know without a doubt that He will never leave us. We can rest our souls on the fact that He is preparing heaven for us where all the raveled ends of life will make sense. This is what we know about the heart of God. It is holy. It is good.

Pray:

Dear heavenly Father, I'm glad You are holy. I don't want that to scare me but to comfort me. I'm glad I can trust You always to be the same and always to be working for my good. I know that You call me to be holy too, and I can't do that without You. As I seek to know You better, please conform me to the image of Jesus so that I can reflect Your heart and so that I will love others and seek their good. I want to be holy like You. In Jesus' name, amen.

THE BEST MIRROR

READ JAMES 1:22–25

Key Verse:

But the man who looks into the perfect mirror of God's law, the law of liberty (or freedom), and makes a habit of so doing, is not the man who sees and forgets. He puts that law into practice and he wins true happiness.
JAMES 1:25 PHILLIPS

Understand:

- What kind of attitude about yourself would cause you to be forgetful of what you've read in God's Word?
- How does seeing yourself in the Bible help you understand God's heart?

Apply:

Have you seen yourself in one of those distorted mirrors in the fun house at the carnival? Or have you caught a glimpse of yourself in a cheap mirror that has become warped or wavy? The images are not flattering.

On the other hand, the best mirror images often are found in fitting rooms. Of course.

The head honchos of the store want you to take home that item—or two or three. They're going to make sure that you like what you see!

God's Word is a mirror that always tells the truth. His law is "perfect," says Psalm 19:7 (ESV). And the apostle James reminded us that this law will give a complete reflection of who we are. It doesn't return to us a hopeless image, nor does it stroke our ego with a flawless resemblance. Instead, it shows us the truth: We are in desperate need of our Savior's help.

Pray:

O God, thank You for providing a mirror for me through Your Word. Because You are truth, You reveal to me the truth about my spiritual condition, my spiritual need, and my spiritual hope! I can trust what You say about the image in the mirror. Today, help me not to forget what You've shown but to obey Your Spirit when He shows me how to fix it. I pray this in Jesus' name. Amen.

MESSY SINKS AND ANXIOUS THOUGHTS

READ 1 PETER 5:6–11

Key Verse:

Casting all your anxieties on him,
because he cares for you.
1 PETER 5:7 ESV

Understand:

- What is in the heart of God that would cause Him to inspire this verse in the Bible?
- How can emptying your cares on Jesus give you peace in your day?

Apply:

One of the easiest jobs in a busy home is to wipe up a messy sink and counter, either in the kitchen or the bathroom. For some reason, it makes the room look cared for, bright, and happy. It takes only a few minutes, yet it's so satisfying.

In our everyday conversations with Jesus, we can seek the heart of God by not allowing little messes to remain in our minds. Each day brings new challenges and worries, and it is easy to shut down the flow of thoughts because we're tired from work or from dealing with relationships or from a headache or from another problem. But instead of putting it off until another day, we need to take out the cloth of trust and wipe it all up and give it to Him. He can help us deal with the prayer requests and the anxiety and the temptations we face.

Pray:

Dear Father in heaven, right now I bring to You the cares of my day. I mop them all up and offer them to You, not a pleasant gift in my eyes, but one that You want me to bring. You ask me to lay before You the anxieties and worries and temptations I face so You can help me deal with them and give me a brighter outlook in return. Thank You, Lord, for loving me enough to want to do that for me. Amen.

THE AROMA OF WORSHIP

READ: PSALM 141:1–4

Key Verse:

Let my prayer be counted as incense before you, and the lifting up of my hands as the evening sacrifice!
PSALM 141:2 ESV

Understand:

- Do we often think only of our side of worship and not what it means to our God?
- Altars in the Old Testament were meaningful places of worship. What do you know about them?

Apply:

For many, walking inside a friend's home to the aroma of a spicy candle is soothing and welcoming. Scent is deeply tied to memories and can trigger visceral responses.

In the Old Testament and still today in some world religions, burning candles and incense is part of bringing an offering to a deity. The pagan nations around ancient Israel often burned incense to their false gods, trying to appease the hostile nature they imagined them to have toward humans. The sensory experience appeals to us as humans; it is a desire that Satan can use against us. He wants us to seek visual verification and to demand things we can see and touch. But we know that our God "does not dwell in houses made by hands" (Acts 7:48 ESV), and so the worship He desires is from the heart. He is not angry with humanity but longs to dwell with us and in us by the presence of His Holy Spirit.

God says we can view our morning prayers to Him as incense rising before His throne. It is pleasant to Him. He welcomes our interaction with Him. He wants to hear our petitions and our praises.

Pray:

O Lord, how wonderful You are! Today, I bring before You my worship. I want it to be a sweet aroma in Your presence. Thank You for the blessings I enjoy, and the best one is that You sent Your own Son to be my Savior. I praise You for that. In Jesus' name, amen.

TOO MUCH BAGGAGE

Read Hebrews 12:1–2

Key Verse:

Wherefore seeing we also are compassed about with so great a cloud of witnesses, let us lay aside every weight, and the sin which doth so easily beset us, and let us run with patience the race that is set before us.

Hebrews 12:1 KJV

Understand:

- What is the longest trip you've taken, and how many bags did you bring with you?
- In your spiritual life, do you carry a lot of baggage?

Apply:

Packing for a trip—love it or hate it. The thought of adventure is exhilarating, and packing is necessary if the trip is longer than a day. Some toss a few essentials into a duffel bag and go on their merry way. Others of us agonize over the selection of each outfit, wanting to have just the right aura for each experience of every day we're gone.

Then, inevitably, there's the return part of the trip when all our lovely imaginations are crumpled in a laundry bag crammed into the suitcase!

If we've traveled very much, we've learned that overpacking can be a problem. While it's great to have a variety of options for the trip, lugging heavy bags into every hotel and fighting with rumpled clothing does not make for an enjoyable trip.

In the adventure of daily life with Christ, there are some things we need not drag along behind us. With the help of the Holy Spirit, we can lay aside those things that would crowd out the enjoyment of the trip and would even tempt us to sin against God.

Pray:

Lord, thank You for the voice of the Holy Spirit that shows me things I need to turn over to You. As I bump up against grievances to be forgiven, worries to be surrendered, thoughts to be conquered, and more, help me quickly give them to You. I love You and trust You today. Amen.

GOD WANTS US TO REST

READ GENESIS 2:1–3

Key Verse:

Then God blessed the seventh day and sanctified it.
GENESIS 2:3 NKJV

Understand:

- Do you plan for regular sleep and for times of leisure? If not, what are the obstacles?
- What if you asked God for His guidance in making a plan for rest and then His help in making it happen? Jot down a few ways you'd like to rest if you could find time.

Apply:

There are times in life when we sacrifice sleep to accomplish a larger goal or to fulfill a responsibility. Losing a little sleep for a night or two won't cause too much damage, other than perhaps causing us to drink too much coffee! But if we make a habit of cheating our bodies of rest and our minds of downtime, we will suffer consequences sooner or later. Researchers have determined that we are more susceptible to illness and depression, among other things, when we are sleep deprived.

Our wise and loving Creator ordained the night hours with us in mind. It wasn't simply to showcase the pearly moon or to give space to the nocturnal animals; it was to gift His crowning creation, human beings, the opportunity to turn off the day and rejuvenate through rest.

God's heart for us is to work and then to rest, to act and then to sleep, to do our best during the day and then to let Him take care of the rest while we sleep.

Pray:

Lord God, You rested on the seventh day of creation and blessed it for us too. You knew that You needed to lead us to rest, that if You left it up to us, we'd fudge. I want to improve in my understanding of rest and in my implementation of it. I ask You to help me find ways to honor You by caring for my body and mind in this way. Amen.

A GOD OF COLOR AND TEXTURE

READ MATTHEW 6:28–30

Key Verses:

> *"Consider the lilies of the field, how they grow: they neither toil nor spin; and yet I say to you that even Solomon in all his glory was not arrayed like one of these."*
>
> MATTHEW 6:28–29 NKJV

Understand:

- Are you tempted to believe the lie that God does not approve of joy and beauty?
- Are you challenged to distinguish biblical self-denial from unbiblical practice?

Apply:

In ancient times, there was a group of people who practiced a form of piety called asceticism. They were sincere, but they were also sincerely wrong. They believed that self-denial was the way to righteousness, that renouncing pleasures and adopting a bleak life would make them holy.

While Christians are called to deny ourselves when our human desires are contrary to God's will, we are not called to live a spartan life merely for the sake of depriving ourselves. There is no glory or holiness in self-imposed pitifulness. We are to bring glory to God by the way we use what He has given.

God created the expanse of the heavens and the silky texture of the rose and the coal-black beady eyes of the eagle and the fluffy magic of snowflakes, and we can sense His love of beauty in how He has created things to delight our senses.

Jesus told the people gathered on a hillside in Judea that they should think about the lilies. This is our reminder, not only that He will take care of us but that He gives us beautiful things to enjoy.

Pray:

Dear Lord, thank You for creating beauty. Thank You that I can seek Your heart in godly ways, and that means that the beauty You created in the natural world can draw me closer to You. Today, help me look around and appreciate what You have created to reflect Your heart. Amen.

THE SHINING OF THE STRONG MAN

READ PSALM 19:1–6

Key Verses:

Of the heavens has God made a tent
for the sun, which is as a bridegroom
coming out of his chamber; and it rejoices
as a strong man to run his course.
PSALM 19:4–5 AMPC

Understand:

- How does the weather affect your mood?
- How does the sun that God created show us His heart toward us?

Apply:

Science tells us that our brains need the sun's light to make the chemicals needed for mental health. The morning light helps set the circadian rhythm of our bodies. The light of the sun assists our cells in making vitamin D. The heat of the sun warms our planet and keeps us from freezing; the sun was placed by God at the exact distance necessary for life to exist. The life-giving properties in sunlight are converted by photosynthesis into nourishment for green plants, which keep animals growing and the cycle of life continuing.

Sometimes we overlook the fact that the physical world our God created gives us vital information about His nature. God designed the sun to nourish life in many ways. The psalmist David was inspired to compare the sun in the sky to a bridegroom, radiant on his wedding day, and to a strong man, primed and ready to run his best race. The sun rejoices to do what it was created to do. What a loving Creator who takes such good care of us!

Pray:

Father God, You have given us all we need to live on this earth, both physically and spiritually. Thank You for the sun in the heavens that reminds me every morning of Your love for me. When I seek to understand Your heart in what I see around me, I see You everywhere. Amen.

GENTLENESS AND STRENGTH ARE IN HIM

READ PSALM 18:31–36

Key Verse:

You have also given me the shield of Your salvation; Your right hand has held me up, Your gentleness has made me great.
PSALM 18:35 NKJV

Understand:

- Do you think of gentleness as greatness? Why or why not?
- What are some areas in your life that could benefit from the gentleness of the Holy Spirit?

Apply:

We teach children to be gentle with puppies and kittens, with baby sisters and brothers, with breakable items, and with others who are hurt or physically challenged. Gentleness is a trait that, incredibly, is shown in the context of strength. Gentleness is strength under control; it is strength restrained; it is deliberate holding back. A person must have inner strength to exhibit gentleness;

simple passivity could be a sign of weakness of character or temperament.

The psalmist David was inspired to write this beautiful psalm; in it he told of both the strength and the gentleness of God, evidenced by divine work in his own life. In the early verses, he described the thundering of the Lord in the heavens, in the sea storms, and in the lightning. And in the verses following, he detailed the rescue of the Lord and His merciful ways toward him.

The heart of our God understands our needs and comes to us, offering both His strength and His gentleness, knowing that we need both.

Pray:

O Lord, I am awed by Your might and also by Your gentle heart. I praise You for who You are and for the way You come to me in my need. I love You, Lord. Your gentleness is at work in me, and I'm thankful. Amen.

THE GOD OF LIFE

READ ISAIAH 44:21–28

Key Verse:

Thus says the LORD, your Redeemer,
who formed you from the womb:
"I am the LORD, who made all things,
who alone stretched out the heavens,
who spread out the earth by myself."
ISAIAH 44:24 ESV

Understand:

- How does an understanding of God as the Creator of all life help us to seek His heart?
- What does this understanding make clear to us about life in the womb?
- For women who have made decisions in the past that they now regret, how can this truth about God help them seek His forgiveness and accept that forgiveness for themselves?

Apply:

From ancient times, humans have worshipped deities who they believed had power over life.

Life is the ultimate victory. To have the power of life and death is to reign. And, unlike silly statues and impotent idols, our God can bring life from nothing. He created all that is from blackness and blankness. He holds the power to give breath and life in His eternal hands.

Pagans of old believed that sacrificing innocent life would appease the gods and thus lengthen their own lives, but our God sacrificed His *own* Son. Jesus laid down His life and shed His blood to buy our eternal life.

In recent times, the power to take life through abortions is the victory many seek. Millions of babies have been sacrificed; millions of mothers have been told not to grieve. But Jesus offers a way back to life for them. The power of life is stronger than the power of death. Because He Himself embodies life.

Pray:

Father in heaven, shine Your light and Your life on our world. Help Your people to stand always for life. Thank You for defeating death for us. Amen.

DAILY TRUTH THAT REACHES THE HEAVENS

Read Psalm 57:7–11

Key Verses:

I will praise You, O Lord, among the peoples;
I will sing to You among the nations.
For Your mercy reaches unto the heavens,
and Your truth unto the clouds.
Psalm 57:9–10 NKJV

Understand:

- Do you feel that it is difficult for people today to find truth in everyday life? Do you trust our sources of information for news and events?
- Does knowing that God is ultimate truth give you comfort or cause you to fear? Why?

Apply:

The history books told the story of the child George Washington and the cherry tree. When he was confronted with a question about whether he chopped it down, he was famously to have said, "I cannot tell a lie." Whether this story is actual fact or legend has been debated. But the fact remains that traditionally there has been a premium put on truth. People valued it.

God not only values truth; He *is* truth. He embodies all that is pure and honest and holy. Jesus said of Himself in John 14:6 (AMPC), "I am the Way and the Truth and the Life." He discussed truth with everyone He met—Nicodemus, the Samaritan woman, Mary and Martha, and even Pilate during His own trial.

God cannot be false to anyone, and we can trust Him. Because He is always steadfast and faithful, we don't have to worry about being deceived or tricked by Him. He is always working for our redemption and our good.

We are not always told the truth in our earthly spheres. News is slanted, advertising is inflated, corporations are underhanded, and appearances are muddled. But God is always true. We can rest our souls on that.

Pray:

O God, You embody truth. I rest in Your steadfast character. Thank You for guiding me into truth by the power of Your Holy Spirit. In Jesus' name, amen.

PUNCTUALITY/TIME

READ DANIEL 2:20–23

Key Verses:

"Blessed be the name of God forever and ever, for wisdom and might are His. And He changes the times and the seasons."
DANIEL 2:20–21 NKJV

Understand:

- Providence refers to the overarching sovereignty of God that is at work in our world. Can you think of an instance when the plans of God worked on your behalf, even if unexpectedly?
- What has helped you learn about this important aspect of His nature?

Apply:

Our God exists out of the reach of time. He transcends it. He chooses to work within it on our behalf, and He created this planet to run by earthly time for our benefit. His timelessness is a part of His being that no human can fully understand. We only know that it is true. If everything about Him were understandable, He would be like us; He wouldn't be God.

In our world, time is important. And many of the things that we pray about are time sensitive, at least in our eyes; but He is not hampered by the calendar nor constrained by the clock.

The prophet Daniel, in this public prayer, was proclaiming the sovereignty of God over everything, even over the times and seasons of kings that He allows in our world. Like us, Daniel knew that was something of which we often need reminded. When we are tempted to doubt, we can seek the heart of God by remembering that He will always work in a way that is good for us. And it will always be right on His time.

Pray:

Thank You, O God, for ruling and reigning in the affairs of this world. We are not on our own; You are in control. Today, I bring my needs to You. They look big and time sensitive, but I choose to believe that You are working out Your plan for me and for those I love. I trust You. Amen.

FIRST THINGS FIRST

READ 1 KINGS 17:8–16

Key Verses:

And Elijah said to her, "Do not fear; go and do as you have said, but make me a small cake from it first, and bring it to me; and afterward make some for yourself and your son. For thus says the LORD *God of Israel: 'The bin of flour shall not be used up, nor shall the jar of oil run dry, until the day the* LORD *sends rain on the earth.'"*

1 KINGS 17:13–14 NKJV

Understand:

- What areas of your life do you find most challenging to prioritize?
- Why would this widow have found it so difficult to feed the prophet first? What have you lost that makes you fearful to trust that God will take care of you when you put Him first?

Apply:

Because we are human and live in a fallen world and are subject to temptation, we struggle at times to keep first things first. In the fast pace of our living and with all the layers of daily existence, it's easy to let the important things fall to the bottom of the pile. Those are the things that matter in eternity but are not urgent in the moment. We forget that every time we don't do these things, we rob ourselves of greater treasure and delight.

Our heavenly Father beckons us to cast our fears into His keeping and to keep first things first. Yes, sometimes there are unexpected contingencies in life that reroute our days and our to-do lists. But, for the ordinary days, let's commit to giving our best energy and most determined effort to what matters most in our relationship with God and with our families.

Pray:

O God, give me wisdom to order my days and my calendar and my to-do list in ways that honor You. Thank You for Your promise to take care of me when I trust You. In Jesus' name, amen.

NO DESTINATION TOO FAR

READ PSALM 139:7–12

Key Verses:

If I take the wings of the morning,
and dwell in the uttermost parts of the
sea, even there Your hand shall lead me,
and Your right hand shall hold me.
PSALM 139:9–10 NKJV

Understand:

- What is your favorite travel destination?
- What kind of topography brings your heart closest to God's heart—the mountains, the oceans, the deserts, the plains, the forests?

Apply:

Most of us can identify with the words of the classic hymn "How Great Thou Art" in our inner response to the world that God made. When we travel to places beyond our own neighborhood, we see once again the sweeping creativity of our Father, who gives us richly all things to enjoy and who is glorified in every tiny creature and in every grain of dirt and bit of leaf. He has designed and ordered this world out of love for us and out of love of beauty. This planet is specially designed for His crowning creation: humankind.

And, in every corner of the earth, His presence abides. There is no destination we can inhabit, by our choice or otherwise, that He is not there. What comfort! Having the confidence that He is reachable from every point of longitude and latitude makes life less fearful, especially in a time when occupations and ministry separate families and keep us apart for periods of time. There is no spot on earth where we need to feel alone. He is there.

Pray:

Dear Father, I am thankful for Your constant presence in this world You have made. There is no better companion than You. Watch over me today, and keep those I love in Your care. In Jesus' name, amen.

CLEANING OUT THE PURSE

READ GALATIANS 5:16–25

Key Verses:

But the fruit of the Spirit is love, joy,
peace, patience, kindness, goodness,
faithfulness, gentleness, self-control;
against such things there is no law.
GALATIANS 5:22–23 ESV

Understand:

- What kinds of things do you carry in your purse or handbag? Is it full of unimportant items?
- Do you need to do a clean-out of your soul and give space to what the Spirit of God wants you to carry with you?

Apply:

Purses are like kitchen tables—they can become cluttered with all manner of unimportant things. They can even become catchalls for the household! "Can you carry this for me?"

Most of the time, we don't mind; but it's necessary to eliminate as much extra stuff as possible so that there is room for the good stuff:

wallet, keys, phone, etc. These are the basics, the things we can't do without as we're out and about.

There are basic items for the Christian life too. Called the fruit of the Spirit, these nine attributes are really reflections of the heart of God. Because these things are His essence, we will reflect them too if we belong to Him. They are the proof that faith in God lives in us, proof of the new life that He has created in us. And they are traits that we continue to grow in as we continue in relationship with Him.

Pray:

Father God, I want to carry the most important things into my day. I want to reflect Your heart as these verses say. I open up my heart to You and ask You to clean out whatever is necessary so that I will have room for You and Your attributes. In Jesus' name, amen.

HEALTHY HOUSEPLANTS AND CONNECTED CHRISTIANS

READ JOHN 15:1–5

Key Verse:

"Abide in me, and I in you. As the branch cannot bear fruit by itself, unless it abides in the vine, neither can you, unless you abide in me."
JOHN 15:4 ESV

Understand:

- Are you a plant lover? How many houseplants do you own?
- What happens to plants that aren't nourished properly?

Apply:

Keeping houseplants is both a pastime and a skill. For all the jokes about "green thumbs," there does seem to be something inexplicable about people who get almost anything to grow and thrive. Perhaps it's in the way they place the plants and water the plants and prune the plants. They simply seem to understand what the plants need.

Jesus, the master communicator, often used everyday illustrations that His listeners and His readers in days to come could identify with. Remember His parables and His illustrative teachings? In this passage in John, Christ compared Himself to the main vine, the trunk, the source of nourishment and life. To continue to live, the branches must be connected to that source.

Houseplants are at the mercy of the housekeeper for their needs of light and nutrition; but as branches connected to Christ, we have daily choices that either keep us connected firmly to Him or begin to sever us from Him. As we seek His heart, we can find daily nourishment and energy, and we'll become beautiful in His care.

Pray:

O Lord, I want my life to be firmly attached to You so that I can be a healthy Christian and bear godly fruit. Thank You for making a way for me to do that through the Bible and the guidance of the Holy Spirit. Amen.

GENERATIONAL BLESSING

READ DEUTERONOMY 7:6–11

Key Verse:

"Know therefore that the LORD *your God is God, the faithful God who keeps covenant and steadfast love with those who love him and keep his commandments, to a thousand generations."*
DEUTERONOMY 7:9 ESV

Understand:

- Is there a godly older woman who speaks truth and blessing into your life?
- How can you become a mentor to a younger woman?

Apply:

The generational support of women is an awesome thing. Having a grandmother or an aunt and most certainly your own mother to come alongside you in life and encourage you in the journey provides strength and courage like nothing else. None of us want to feel like we're alone in this thing. And none of us want to feel like the challenges we're facing and the emotions we're feeling have never been experienced by anyone else. We don't want to feel weird and isolated.

God made women relational in a different way than He designed men. And that's good. We're supposed to be beautifully different from each other. But He also created the family so that we could have the support of other women, not to alienate us from men but so we could have better relationships with them.

Ask God to help you fill that gap for a younger woman; if she's younger than you and a few years behind you in life season, you qualify! Encourage her in the truth that God is faithful and keeps His covenant and that He will be with her until the end.

Pray:

Lord, I want to be a blessing to others as those in my life have blessed me. Show me how, and open up doors for me and guide me as I walk through them. Amen.

THINKING ABOUT THE FUTURE

Read Isaiah 25:8–9

Key Verse:

> *He will swallow up death forever;*
> *and the Lord God will wipe away*
> *tears from all faces, and the reproach of*
> *his people he will take away from all*
> *the earth, for the Lord has spoken.*
> Isaiah 25:8 esv

Understand:

- Do you cry easily, or do you find it difficult to show emotion in front of others?
- When you think about the future, do you battle fear over what might happen?

Apply:

The common idea of women crying when they are stressed or upset is often true, but it is often not true too. Because women are deeply relational and, on the average, more aware of their emotions and sensitive to how everyday happenings affect them, we are prone to release those emotions in observable ways. However, there are many women who, while sharply feeling emotional pain, do not let it show on the outside. There is variety among us.

Whatever our personal temperament may be, though, most of us can confess that thinking of the future causes a bit of mental anxiety. We don't know what will happen and to whom it will happen, and we don't know how we will handle what happens. But our God tells us to trust His good heart. He doesn't promise that He will isolate us from the human life that all of us lead and from the bad things that can happen in that life, but He does assure us that He will be with us and redeem us in the midst of it and that someday He will wipe away all the tears from our faces. Let's think of that as we contemplate the future. No death and no tears and a spirit of gladness sound like heaven.

Pray:

Lord God, I choose today to look at the future through Your promises. Thank You for being with me in the sad and stressful times, and thank You for heaven ahead of me. Amen.

GET THE LOOK

READ ROMANS 8:28–31

Key Verse:

For whom He foreknew, He also predestined to be conformed to the image of His Son, that He might be the firstborn among many brethren.
ROMANS 8:29 NKJV

Understand:

- Are you a fashion-trend follower? Why or why not?
- How does the knowledge that Christ is conforming you to His image give you confidence in your spiritual life?

Apply:

We are told that there is a difference between classic style and fashion trends and seasonal fads. There are those pieces that are ageless, that seamlessly glide from one decade to the next and the next and always look appropriate and in good taste. And then there are those items that have the shape of current trends and reflect the silhouette that is presently thought to be attractive. And finally, there are those faddish accessories and articles of apparel that everyone wants to wear for a few months and then are found languishing in the thrift stores.

The very idea of fashion is conformity to prevailing thought and alignment with popular ideas. This is not wrong in and of itself, but it can become wrong if we do it for reasons of image and pride and disregard the restraints of economy and modesty and charity.

But in the life that God is working in us, being conformed to His image is always a good thing. It is always in style in heaven for Christ followers to look like Him.

Pray:

Lord Jesus, I want to look like You so that when others see me or spend time around me, they will know that I belong to You and Your Spirit in me will draw them toward You too. Guide me today and conform me to Your likeness. In Your name I pray. Amen.

LEARNING AND GROWING

READ EPHESIANS 4:13–16

Key Verses:

We are not meant to remain as children at the mercy of every chance wind of teaching and the jockeying of men who are expert in the craft presentation of lies. But we are meant to hold firmly to the truth in love, and to grow up in every way into Christ, the head.
EPHESIANS 4:14–15 PHILLIPS

Understand:

- Is there a hobby or skill that you enjoy learning about?
- As a godly woman, what are you doing to increase your lifelong learning about Him?

Apply:

Most of us couldn't wait to graduate high school—and then college, if that was our life path. We wanted to be free of homework and assignments and grades and classrooms. We looked forward to getting on with real life.

Aside from the fact that real life still has

challenges and restrictions, our younger selves also may not have considered that there is a certain joy in learning. In fact, learning new information and new skills and new routines can be pleasurable and fulfilling. The happiest people are lifelong learners, the ones who approach life with curious minds and eager hearts.

The apostle Paul was inspired to write to the Ephesian Christians about growth in Christ. Like them, we are meant by God to continue learning and doing and being until someday, in His presence, we will be complete and ready for eternity. It is our responsibility to look for opportunities to learn, to put ourselves under good biblical preaching, and to associate ourselves with a faithful Christian community. If we do, we will discover the delight of learning more about Him.

Pray:

Heavenly Father, I want always to keep growing. Let me not have a withered mind or a stale outlook. Help me put myself in situations and relationships that spur me on to growth in grace. In Jesus' name, amen.

THE GIFT OF TIME

READ GENESIS 1:1–5

Key Verse:

In the beginning, God created
the heavens and the earth.
GENESIS 1:1 ESV

Understand:

- Do you use a daily to-do list or a weekly to-do list or both?
- How does God's creation of time and space bless us every day?

Apply:

We don't know if ancient peoples used lists, but most of us use them today! It was probably not practical for them to scratch their tasks on stone tablets or write them on papyrus scrolls or parchment paper. For that matter, most people in biblical times couldn't write and neither could common folk for much of the centuries that followed. So, even if they'd wanted to keep a checklist, they couldn't have accomplished it. Perhaps their lives were simpler then; but then again, people have always had a lot to do, and people are people in any generation.

The Bible doesn't record that God had a to-do list. We know that He carefully crafted and executed His creation strategy and that there was an order to it. He established a world of beauty and order. It was only after the entrance of sin into our plane that the laws of death and decay and destruction entered.

One of the gifts that God created for human beings is the boundaries of time. We often wish for more hours in our days; but He, the wise Lord and Creator, knows what is best. And as we acknowledge Him in how we spend time, He will help us spend it with wisdom.

Pray:

Creator God, You do all things well, and You created time limits in our days and weeks and months and years for our good. Today, help me use well the hours I have. In Jesus' name, amen.

EMOTIONAL STRENGTH

Read Deuteronomy 33:26–29

Key Verses:

There is none like unto the God of Jeshurun, who rideth upon the heaven in thy help, and in his excellency on the sky. The eternal God is thy refuge, and underneath are the everlasting arms.

Deuteronomy 33:26–27 KJV

Understand:

- What makes you feel emotionally strong?
- Does the promise of the eternal God to be with you change your perspective on the big challenge facing you today? How?

Apply:

Emotional stamina is more accessible to some personalities and some brains. The way our temperaments work and our minds process information is unique and complex. It's a fact that some break quicker than others. Part of this can be attributed to physical and mental health, personal background, and present life situations. Being a Christian does not guarantee that a person will be emotionally healthy. But it does fortify our minds with the strength of God's Word and the assurance that He is with us.

An old gospel song spoke of "standing on the promises." Indeed, that is a strength tactic of Christians down through the centuries. Remember that former generations of Christ followers didn't have it so easy either. They faced martyrdom, imprisonment, political ostracization, public humiliation, and more.

As you look at your day, look also at the heart of God, who promises to be your courage and conviction and calm. There is none like Him. And His arms of refuge are everlasting.

Pray:

O God, I bring to You my needs and my thoughts. I surrender to You my doubts and my fears. Be my strength today. In Jesus' name, amen.

THE MORNING ROUTINE

READ AMOS 5:8–9

Key Verse:

He made the Pleiades and Orion;
He turns the shadow of death into
morning and makes the day dark as night;
He calls for the waters of the sea and
pours them out on the face of the earth.
AMOS 5:8 NKJV

Understand:

- Are you a morning person?
- How do the light and hope of morning remind us of their Creator?

Apply:

For many of us, fresh coffee poured into a waiting mug is a reward for swinging our feet out of bed and greeting the day's responsibilities. This fragrant ritual lures us to go at life again.

But for the one who understands the promise of each morning and the Maker of every single morning that has ever been, there is more to a new day than the brew from the coffee bean.

God loves order and steady faithfulness, and

He made our sun to mirror that attribute of His. It rises in the east every morning and sets in the west every evening. It is steady; it does not falter. And as the night stars cover themselves and slide to the opposite hemisphere, the streaks of pink daylight filter through to remind us again that there is hope and there is a new beginning.

As wonderful as it is, coffee doesn't really wake us up every morning. No, that is our faithful God, whose steady presence infuses us with more energy than a cup of joe ever did.

Pray:

O Lord, thank You for creating the cycle of day and night and for offering me fresh grace every morning. As I seek Your heart this day, I rest in the knowledge that You will be there for my tomorrow too. Amen.

PAIN AND DISEASE AND ETERNAL KNOWLEDGE

READ COLOSSIANS 3:1–4

Key Verses:

Give your heart to the heavenly things,
not to the passing things of earth. For, as far as
this world is concerned, you are already dead,
and your true life is a hidden one in Christ.
COLOSSIANS 3:2–3 PHILLIPS

Understand:

- What diseases run in your family? Cancer? Heart disease? Diabetes? Autoimmune disorders?
- How are you dealing with either the possibility or the reality of disease and all the complications and fears it brings?

Apply:

One of the hardest circumstances in life is chronic illness and pain. In our fallen world, we and those we love often are plagued by conditions and diagnoses that assault our comfort and complicate our lives. And beyond that, they threaten to snatch precious years off our time on earth. This is not easy to accept. We enjoy our homes and families, and the thought of being separated from them, understandably, makes us sad.

So, it is good to remind ourselves that our real lives, our true lives, are yet to come. Especially when the culture of this present world runs after temporary glamor and fame and comfort, it is right for us to recall that the things of this earth are passing but the things of God are eternal.

Our God will someday make all things new, even a new heaven and earth. He will banish disease and eradicate pain and give us perfect bodies and minds. Until then, we can live in the promise of that redemption.

Pray:

Lord, please be with me in the physical challenges I face and bless those in my family who today are fighting chronic pain. Thank You for the reality that someday things will be different. I look forward to that day. Amen.

THE INVESTMENT OF CLEANSING

Read 2 Corinthians 5:16–21

Key Verses:

For if a man is in Christ he becomes a new person altogether—the past is finished and gone, everything has become fresh and new. All this is God's doing, for he has reconciled us to himself through Jesus Christ; and he has made us agents of the reconciliation.

2 Corinthians 5:17–18 PHILLIPS

Understand:

- Would you toss out a favorite garment that had a bad stain, or would you keep looking for a remedy?
- If we put forth time and expense to clean a piece of clothing, how much more energy would God expend to redeem us?

Apply:

Our grandmothers or great-grandmothers had "wash day," but for most of us, it's laundry day every day. With washing machines and tumble dryers, electric irons and steamers, the job is much easier to complete. Even removing stains has gotten easier with the array of stain removers at the store. But what's still needed at times is a bit of elbow grease—good, old-fashioned scrubbing.

Maybe it's mustard or chocolate or mud, but redeeming a cherished piece of clothing from a stubborn stain calls for investment. Making it fresh and new tests our commitment despite the inconvenience.

God, in Christ, wanted to make us new. He was willing to send His own Son to blot out our transgressions and restore us to beauty. The price was not too high for His great love for us.

We are trophies of grace because of Him. We were soiled souls who could not cleanse ourselves, but through His investment on our behalf, we can stand clean before Him.

Pray:

Father God, I am thankful that You were willing to send Jesus to make me clean in Your sight. You loved me so much that You wanted to redeem me and restore my relationship with You. Thank You. I love You. Amen.

KNOWLEDGE OF SPARROWS AND STRANDS

Read Matthew 10:28–33

Key Verses:

"Two sparrows sell for a farthing,
don't they? Yet not a single sparrow falls
to the ground without your Father's
knowledge. The very hairs of your head are
all numbered. Never be afraid, then—
you are far more valuable than sparrows."
Matthew 10:29–31 PHILLIPS

Understand:

- Have you ever tried to count the strands of hair on your head?
- If God knows the number of hair strands you had this morning and the number you have right now, how many other details does He have up-to-the-minute knowledge of?

Apply:

When we say that God is all-knowing, it sounds great and true, but it doesn't really sink into our understanding until we think about all the extrapolations of that truth. Jesus tried to help us understand with the example about the sparrows and the hairs of our heads.

According to some statistics, house sparrows are the most common bird in the world. And yet Jesus assured us that the Creator God knows every time one of them misses the branch or is shot down.

Likewise, there are thousands of strands of hair on our heads, and still God knows an exact count on every single head on every single continent on this planet. That is all-knowing. That is our God. He knows every tiny detail and nuance about you. And today, He wants to work in your life for good and He wants to comfort you while He does.

Trust His heart. Believe His words. Reach out for His embrace.

Pray:

Heavenly Father, I'm grateful for Your knowledge of me. I lift up to You my problems and my anxious thoughts. Work in my personality and in my mind and in my family; You know all of these things so well. Thank You. In Jesus' name, amen.

OUR STEADFAST GOD

READ JAMES 1:13–18

Key Verse:

But every good endowment that we possess and every complete gift that we have received must come from above, from the Father of all lights, with whom there is never the slightest variation or shadow of inconsistency.

JAMES 1:17 PHILLIPS

Understand:

- Is it a virtue to be changeable, to evolve in perspective and opinion?
- How does the shifting moral landscape remind us that we don't need a God who changes His mind but one who remains steadfast and sure?

Apply:

Have you worked with someone who is bull-headed and always "right"? It's likely more pleasant to have a colleague who is open to changing their mind if credible information comes along that merits it. But what we like in others, we wouldn't want in our God.

As human beings, we don't have perfect understanding of people, situations, and concepts. We do indeed learn more about people and circumstances, and as our perception changes, so does our viewpoint and so do our convictions.

But God has known everything perfectly from eternity past. He will never have an information gap, and He will never forget a minor detail. Because He has complete knowledge, He always has the right viewpoint of whatever is happening.

The Bible tells us that this 100 percent correct viewpoint is matched by His absolute holiness and by His unchanging love. The theologians call God's universal understanding omniscience. As His children, we can rest in His unchangeableness. And in the goodness that goes with it.

Pray:

Dear Lord, sometimes I have to change my mind, but You never change Your mind on sin and redemption and love for the whole world. Thank You for loving me steadfastly. In Jesus' name, amen.

FEEDING OTHERS

READ JOHN 6:35–40

Key Verse:

> *Jesus said to them, "I am the bread of life; whoever comes to me shall not hunger, and whoever believes in me shall never thirst."*
>
> JOHN 6:35 ESV

Understand:

- Do you remember going to church dinners as a child?
- How does the church's fondness for feeding people point to the food that Jesus gives?

Apply:

Potluck dinners. Fish frys. Chili suppers. Ice cream socials. All of these have been hosted by local churches wanting to fellowship with their members and to bring new people into the gathering.

Many of us remember going to food events in our home churches, and we loved them. Religious people are sometimes criticized for always having food at their activities, but there are probably several reasons for why food is prevalent.

- Food expresses care and gives comfort.
- Food is a nonthreatening way to bring people together who might not otherwise come inside a church.
- Food nourishes the belly, which points to the nourishment of life that Jesus offers.

When the church feeds people, it is operating in kind with its Head, the Lord Jesus. He fed hungry people while He walked the earth, and before His crucifixion, He broke bread and reminded His disciples that His body was going to be broken for their eternal nourishment. God and His people feed others. He is not the God of skimpy rations but the God of abundance for those who are hungry, both physically and spiritually. As His children, we are to nourish others too, as they search for something to satisfy their soul hunger. And we are to point them to Him, the only one who can truly satisfy.

Pray:

Lord God, Your life-giving nature shows me how I need to interact with others today. I want my words and my attitude to provide nourishment for those I come in contact with. I ask You to give me the opportunity. In Jesus' name, amen.

THE GIFT OF SONG

READ EXODUS 15:1–2

Key Verse:

"The LORD *is my strength and my song,*
and he has become my salvation."
EXODUS 15:2 ESV

Understand:

- Do you sing when things are bad?
- In times of crisis and joy and simple routine, what does the joy of the Lord do for us?

Apply:

Some of us sing in the shower. Some of us sing in the rain. Some of us sing when we're alone and frightened.

The Bible tells of those who sang at various times in their lives. Paul and Silas sang at midnight after being beaten and imprisoned. Moses and the people of Israel sang after the Red Sea closed up on their enemies. These stories and others remind us that a song in our hearts and on our lips gives us both strength and joy.

If you've ever seen footage of the way singing

is produced in the vocal cords, you know it's an astonishing sight. The vocal folds flutter and quiver, giving the effect of fragile butterfly wings. The sound from inside the body is a gliding sort of murmuring, very different from the sound on the outside. But the God of heaven, who could have chosen to create us with any kind of ability He desired, thought the ability to make beautiful sound was important. He gave us the gift of song.

In our low moments and in our high moments, we can get close to the heart of God by offering back to Him the gift of song. He comes close as we lift our human voices to His divine throne.

Pray:

Creator God, thank You for giving me the ability to sing and for the songs You help me offer back to You. May I never forget that both strength and joy are found in singing to You. Amen.

ORPHANS NO MORE

READ JOHN 14:15–18

Key Verse:

"I will not leave you as orphans;
I will come to you."
JOHN 14:18 ESV

Understand:

- Since you were small, how many close friends have you had?
- Because the Holy Spirit is not only to be *with* us but to be *in* us, what does that say about the relationship He will have with us? How can we benefit from it?

Apply:

Many children's stories of old centered on an orphan who experienced hard times and then found love and belonging. Perhaps this was because in bygone days, orphans were considered inferior in worth. Maybe it was because poverty in those times contributed to a lack of medical care for ailing parents and to the mortality rate in mothers giving birth. Maybe it was because unwed mothers were the most likely to give up their children for adoption and society blamed the child for the parents' irresponsibility. But, whatever the reason, orphans were unwanted and unloved.

Jesus promised His followers that He would not leave them without comfort, as a parent abandoning a child, but that He would send someone to abide with them—the Holy Spirit. Since He could indwell every believer, this was much better than Jesus being in only one place with a small group of followers.

Perhaps you have not had many close friends. Maybe you're a loner. Maybe you've been abandoned. Maybe you feel isolated and bereft. But, if you are a child of God, the Holy Spirit will never leave you. Don't fear that you will ever be alone. He abides.

Pray:

Lord Jesus, thank You for sending the comforter. Thank You that I am not a spiritual orphan. Thank You for abiding with me. Amen.

PEACE AND WAR

READ JOHN 16:31–33

Key Verse:

"I have said these things to you, that in me you may have peace. In the world you will have tribulation. But take heart; I have overcome the world."
JOHN 16:33 ESV

Understand:

- Do you have family members who have fought in wars or are currently serving in a military conflict?
- Jesus is called the Prince of Peace. When do you think that promise will be fulfilled?

Apply:

Civilizations have been fighting wars since practically the beginning of time. The very first conflict we read about on planet earth was between two brothers, Cain and Abel. And ever since, peoples have risen against peoples and tried to conquer each other.

While we understand that there are times

when a nation must defend herself and her people, we know that death on the battlefield, indeed death of any kind, was not God's plan for the world. And so, we look ahead with hope to the day when Jesus will ride from heaven on a white horse and bring peace to the nations—not a false, manipulated peace, but a real peace that will fulfill the scriptures and give the land rest.

The heart of our God wants us to know peace. As we seek to know Him better, we can understand a little more about how much He hates sin and why. Sin is the destructive force behind every evil, painful thing in this world. And God wants to protect us from its mushroom cloud of evil. Only as we allow Him to reign in our souls will we really know the meaning of peace.

Pray:

Thank You, God of heaven, that You are greater than the wars of this land and have more power than any earthly army. And yet, You care about conflicts we have and pain we experience. Today, let me look at this planet through Your eyes and rest in the peace You give. In Jesus' name, amen.

THE INNER ENERGY

READ 2 CORINTHIANS 4:15–18

Key Verses:

This is the reason why we never collapse. The outward man does indeed suffer wear and tear, but every day the inward man receives fresh strength. These little troubles (which are really so transitory) are winning for us a permanent, glorious and solid reward out of all proportion to our pain.
2 CORINTHIANS 4:16–17 PHILLIPS

Understand:

- Is your temperament naturally optimistic or pessimistic?
- How can an eternal perspective on the God of heaven help us have a positive mindset as we live our lives?

Apply:

Theologians often say that God is not up in heaven wringing His hands. And it is true. There has never been an earthly or heavenly problem that He could not solve. Nothing that happens in the universe is surprising to Him. No storm or tragedy or battle on earth is too big for Him to bring us through.

Seeking to understand the heart of God means that we get up close to Him and try to gain His perspective on life and eternity. Of course, we will never understand things as He does; we are finite and we will remain finite, even in heaven. He is infinite, and He cannot be contained, cannot be explained, cannot be overcome and dismissed. He fills all and is in all. His glory fills the universe and the heavens.

The apostle Paul wrote to the Corinthian Christians that He was the reason why they did not collapse and lose heart. The inner person is being renewed daily by the God of the universe, who never runs out of energy or grace for His children. What a God we serve!

Pray:

O Lord, I can't live this life without You, but with You I can endure all things. Thank You for being in control and for helping me overcome in Your name. Amen.

FOUNTAINS AND BUBBLING SPRINGS

READ JOHN 4:10–14

Key Verses:

Jesus answered and said to her,
"Whoever drinks of this water will thirst
again, but whoever drinks of the water
that I shall give him will never thirst.
But the water that I shall give him
will become in him a fountain of water
springing up into everlasting life."
JOHN 4:13–14 NKJV

Understand:

- Do you like fountains?
- How does the imagery of a fountain show us the abundance of life that Jesus brings?

Apply:

Fountains conjure up images of calm and opulence. They are found in business buildings and luxury hotels. They stand guard at memorials and in city parks. They mesmerize children and adults alike.

Fountains today give the impression that the water supply is unending. It never stops. Recycled through the fountain's mechanisms, it keeps going and going.

The modern fountain was not the mental image that the Samaritan woman would have envisioned, however. For her, it would have been a spring, bubbling up deep from an underground source, a rich and inexhaustible supply of life-giving water. And this is what Jesus told her would be the source of her life if she trusted in Him.

Our God is a fount of never-ending, life-giving water for the soul. In Him, we find the mercy and grace and redemption to fill us up and give us abundant life, both here and for eternity.

Pray:

Dear Lord, I praise You for the abundance I discover in You. Though millions have drawn on Your supply, You never run out. Thank You for being the fountain of life for me. Amen.

THE LIVING WORD

Read Psalm 119:54–60

Key Verses:

Your statutes have been my songs in the house of my pilgrimage. I remember Your name in the night, O Lord, and I keep Your law.
Psalm 119:54–55 NKJV

Understand:

- What is your favorite genre of book to read?
- The Word of God has stories and commandments and wise sayings and history and prophecy and admonition and much more. In what way has God been speaking to you recently?

Apply:

The Word of God is living and powerful. It is no ordinary book. It has the ability to slice through to the soul and to reveal the hidden things in the heart.

The psalmist recorded his thoughts and meditations on the law of God. He revered it highly and told his readers how the words had become songs for him and a remembrance in the night.

Some people feel more comfortable consulting their feelings about a certain matter rather than digging in to the Bible to see God's opinion. They hold that if they do not "feel" condemned in their conscience, then that is the last word. Sadly, this is not the case. God's law transcends our feelings. If He has spoken on it in His Word, we need not spend time asking Him for an opinion. He has already given it.

We need to open our minds and hearts to the Book that reveals the heart and mind of God. It is His gift to us to help us in all we do.

Pray:

O Lord God, Your Word is holy and true. Thank You for providing it for our instruction and guidance. Help me understand its precepts and honor its teachings. In Jesus' name, amen.

THE ROYAL WAY

READ PSALM 47:5–9

Key Verses:

Sing praises to God, sing praises! Sing praises to our King, sing praises! For God is the King of all the earth; sing praises with understanding.

PSALM 47:6–7 NKJV

Understand:

- Have you ever been in the presence of royalty?
- How does our understanding of royals on earth inform our view of God, the King of all?

Apply:

The world is fascinated with royal lives—what they wear and what they eat, where they vacation and how they spend their free time. There are reporters who follow them and photographers who hound them. There is fanfare wherever they go and squads of protection around them. Their favor is sought and their judgment respected, even if they're not the favorite monarch. What they think matters to the average person in the kingdom.

God is a king—the King over all the earth. He has more power than any earthly royal, and His throne has been established from before time began. He reigns over the inhabitants of heaven and earth, the seas and the firmament, and anywhere and everywhere in this universe. He is supreme, and every living thing knows it but man.

Nature does what nature is supposed to do. The animal kingdom does what it is supposed to do. Only man and woman are puffed up by pride and rebellion to go against God's plan for them.

But anywhere that human beings acknowledge the truth and welcome Him in, there is festivity and belonging and celebration that not even the royals could match!

Pray:

Lord, as I seek to know Your heart, I want to acknowledge You as King of the universe and King of my heart. Get glory from my surrendered life today. In Jesus' name, amen.

RENOVATIONS AND REDEMPTION

READ 2 CORINTHIANS 3:12–18

Key Verses:

Now the Lord is the Spirit; and where the Spirit of the Lord is, there is liberty. But we all, with unveiled face, beholding as in a mirror the glory of the Lord, are being transformed into the same image from glory to glory, just as by the Spirit of the Lord.
2 CORINTHIANS 3:17–18 NKJV

Understand:

- Have you ever renovated a home?
- Being transformed is a little like renovation, but it goes beyond. What lives have you seen transformed by the power of Christ?

Apply:

There is a little spark of God's love of redemption inside human beings. We are drawn to stories of transformation. House flipping and vintage car restoration and upcycling are all trends that point to the magic we feel when something is made new and returned to beautiful condition.

But long before the first home renovation took place, God was planning redemption. His heart could not let His creation be separated from Him for eternity. And so He paid the cost of the repairs out of His heavenly treasure. He sent His best, His only Son, to pay the high price.

His willingness to let His beloved Son suffer and die for those who didn't appreciate Him reveals His nature. This is the core of His heart. He is love. And to seek His heart truly, we must acknowledge His sacrifice and surrender our own lives back to Him. Only in relationship with Him can we begin to fathom even a small fraction of how much He loves us.

Pray:

Father, I could never repay You, and You don't want me to. Instead, You want to show me Your heart and have a relationship with me, both now and for eternity. Thank You for Your work of renovation in my soul. Thank You for redeeming me with the blood of Jesus. Amen.

THE MEANING OF HIS NAME

READ EXODUS 3:14–17

Key Verse:

God said also to Moses, This shall you say to the Israelites: The Lord, the God of your fathers, of Abraham, of Isaac, and of Jacob, has sent me to you! This is My name forever, and by this name I am to be remembered to all generations.

EXODUS 3:15 AMPC

Understand:

- Do you like your name? Why or why not?
- What does the name that God gives to Himself tell us about Him?

Apply:

Few people actually like their given name. Most would choose a different one if they were the ones choosing and not their parents. We might choose something more glamorous and less homely or more common and less unique. And many people would change their last name if they could do it without causing problems for their family. We're usually not thrilled with our names.

But the God of heaven is satisfied with His name. It fits Him perfectly. In fact, He has many names, which all point to His deity and His essence and His nature. In this instance, He told Moses to refer to Him as the God of Abraham, Isaac, and Jacob. These men, though respected by the people of Israel, were all now dead! But God was telling the Jewish people that they were still living, for He is not the God of the dead but of the living. Whatever He comes into contact with He makes alive. And through Moses, He was going to make alive the nation of Israel once more.

As you read His Word and talk to Him today, think about the names of God and what they tell us about Him and His work in the world and in us. Thank Him for His mercy and love and the life He brings.

Pray:

Dear God, I'm glad I know the God of the living, the God whose names perfectly define Him and in whose heart I can trust. I pray this in Jesus' name. Amen.

HIGHEST OF ALL

READ COLOSSIANS 1:13–18

Key Verse:

He also is the Head of [His] body, the church; seeing He is the Beginning, the Firstborn from among the dead, so that He alone in everything and in every respect might occupy the chief place [stand first and be preeminent].
COLOSSIANS 1:18 AMPC

Understand:

- What rank are you in the birth order of the home you grew up in?
- Whether you are the firstborn or not, what do you know about the feeling of responsibility in a firstborn child?

Apply:

In ancient times, the role of the firstborn child was one of great respect and great responsibility. With the deference shown to them also came the weight of the family. The firstborn male would have the privilege of inheriting the family ownings and carrying on the family name. He would be responsible for the care of his aging parents. He was greatly honored but greatly burdened.

Jesus is the firstborn, the only begotten Son of God. The Bible has referred to Him as our elder brother. He is also called the firstborn of the living, since God raised Him to life so that we might also live.

Jesus had the responsibility of our lives on His hands. He paid the price for our salvation and then ascended to His Father. On the cross of Calvary, He took time to say, "It's done; I completed what You gave Me to do." The weight of His burden for us, we could not carry. But He took it and gave us life instead. And now, He is head of the church and the preeminent one. He did what only He could do. And we are the grateful recipients.

Pray:

Father God, I can only say that I am grateful for Your love for me and for Jesus' willing sacrifice for my sin. I want to bear my responsibility well as I live for You. Give me wisdom to do that today. Amen.

ADDICTIONS AND OUR TRIUMPH THROUGH CHRIST

Read Psalm 116:5–9

Key Verses:

For You have delivered my life from death, my eyes from tears, and my feet from stumbling and falling. I will walk before the Lord in the land of the living.
Psalm 116:8–9 AMPC

Understand:

- What addictions have you dealt with in your family and community?
- How have you found deliverance from addiction (whether physical or mental)?

Apply:

Addiction to substances is a result of the awfulness of sin in our world. People who become enslaved by unhealthy bodily hungers may be dealing with contributing factors of which we are unaware. God is the ruler over all the earth, but He does not forcibly keep people from making unwise and even sinful choices. And so, when people make decisions to live in darkness, the Lord will allow them that freedom even though it will destroy them.

But the heart of our God wants to deliver captives. He reaches out with His love and mercy. Sometimes people respond and sometimes they don't. Sometimes they continue stumbling along, turning to other things for help and rescue. But nothing will help us triumph over addiction like Jesus!

Pray:

Thank You, O God, for Your redemption and grace, for loving me and drawing me to You. Thank You that I can point others to You, knowing that You will set them free for Your glory. Amen.

MISSIONS AND THE BREAD OF LIFE

READ JOHN 6:33–40

Key Verse:

This is My Father's will and His purpose, that everyone who sees the Son and believes in and cleaves to and trusts in and relies on Him should have eternal life, and I will raise him up [from the dead] at the last day.
JOHN 6:40 AMPC

Understand:

- Do you pray for people around the world and for the missions' organizations trying to reach them?
- How can seeing Jesus as the bread of life for a spiritually hungry world help us be more intentional about praying and giving to missions?

Apply:

We are accustomed to hearing the terms "first world" and "third world" when referring to wealthy nations and poor nations, respectively. The term "second world" was also used by the

United Nations in 1945 when defining countries in terms of economic status.

God sees only "the world" whom He loved and for whom He sent His Son—not for the planet itself, the terra firma, but for the peoples of that planet. Destitute or affluent, people everywhere need Jesus. Yet, we recognize that the masses in poorer countries do not have the same advantages of travel and media and literature that others enjoy, and so their access to gospel messaging is often limited.

The heart of our Father in heaven is that everyone would come to trust in His Son's death for their salvation and begin a relationship with Him. As we seek to know our God, we will share His compassion and yearning for lost souls. And it will inspire us to pray and to contribute as we are able.

Pray:

O God, thank You for loving the peoples of the world and for making the bread of life available to all who turn to You. Help me do my part in bringing the gospel light to those who do not know. In Jesus' name, amen.

GOD OF DELIVERANCE

READ PSALM 32:7–11

Key Verse:

You are a hiding place for me;
you preserve me from trouble; you surround
me with shouts of deliverance.
PSALM 32:7 ESV

Understand:

- Are you a person who regularly misplaces her keys?
- Thinking about the relief you feel when something lost is found, what kind of relief is felt when God delivers His children from larger problems?

Apply:

Losing keys is frustrating and frightening. It uses up time spent in searching, and it creates panic about the possibility of them not being located. Since keys are our way to enter essential places, misplacing them puts our lives on hold. Some people have extra keys hidden or an extra set of keys in a specific place for just such an emergency. However, there is still the thought that someone may find the missing keys and use them against us in some way.

God holds the keys to our deliverance, our eternal deliverance, which is of far greater importance than the relief we feel at finding our keys. He is the only one who can deliver us from eternal death and preserve us when we are in trouble.

The psalmist mentions God's instruction and steadfast love and the joy we can find in Him. He preserves those who trust in Him. He delivers them and gives them the promise of future rest from all their troubles.

Pray:

Lord God, I can't count the times You have delivered me from my daily troubles, all the small things I bring to You and all the big things that happen too. Thank You that Your heart toward me is one of deliverance and steadfast love. Amen.

THE TRANSFORMATIVE GOD

READ PHILIPPIANS 3:14–21

Key Verses:

But our citizenship is in heaven, and from it we await a Savior, the Lord Jesus Christ, who will transform our lowly body to be like his glorious body, by the power that enables him even to subject all things to himself.

PHILIPPIANS 3:20–21 ESV

Understand:

- What do you look forward to experiencing in heaven someday?
- How can the apostle's words about the transformation of our bodies help us understand the power of God at work even now in us and in our world?

Apply:

Looking in the mirror every morning reminds us that we have lowly bodies! They are subject to the laws of deterioration: aging, sagging, wrinkling, graying, and all the rest. But the Bible promises that we will someday have bodies like Jesus' body: ageless and eternal, perfect and lasting forever.

While we live here, we notice other things that need to be changed as well. Everything around us needs the redeeming touch of our God. And because we know that He is at work in our eternity and He tells the truth, we have the faith to believe that He will fix all the problems that face us, in His time. Since He is able to resurrect and to have all things in subjection under His feet, we know that He can do all the other things that need His hand on them.

Every ordinary day is a chance to allow Him to bring us one step closer to the glory that awaits. His very essence is completion and perfection, and He will work that in us, one day at a time, until that day when we see Him face-to-face.

Pray:

Dear Father, Your work in me goes on, and I welcome that. Thank You that You never leave anything unfinished. Amen.

THE GOD OF SINGING

READ ZEPHANIAH 3:17–20

Key Verse:

"The LORD *your God is in your midst, a mighty one who will save; he will rejoice over you with gladness; he will quiet you by his love; he will exult over you with loud singing."*

ZEPHANIAH 3:17 ESV

Understand:

- Have you ever been serenaded?
- God tells us that He will sing over His people, Israel. What does this tell us about His nature?

Apply:

In order to understand our God, we have to remember that He is in a covenant with the people of Israel. This is not because they are better than another ethnicity. Because of the faith of Abraham, God promised that his descendants would be as innumerable as the sands of the sea and that all the nations of the earth would be blessed through his descendants—literally, the Messiah, who was born of Jewish ancestry.

The covenant that God made with Abraham because of his faithful choice to believe God continues to this day. God will never forsake Israel. He will fight for her and bring her again into relationship with Him someday when she recognizes Jesus as her true Messiah.

If you are a Gentile (non-Jewish) believer, you are not left out of this wonderful picture of God singing. Because we know that His heart rejoices in those who love and trust Him, we understand that He welcomes all people into His family and that the promises of redemption and relationship that He made to Israel are, because of the death of Jesus, open to us as well.

Today, believe that He loves you because He told you so. And He cannot lie.

Listen for the sound of singing in your soul. And rejoice in His care.

Pray:

O Lord, the thought that You rejoice to be in relationship with me is a comfort and strength. Thank You for providing a way for me to be with You always. I praise You today. Amen.

FORGIVING FATHER

READ PSALM 103:6–14

Key Verses:

As far as the east is from the west,
so far does he remove our transgressions
from us. As a father shows compassion
to his children, so the LORD *shows*
compassion to those who fear him.
PSALM 103:12–13 ESV

Understand:

- What is the best earthly story of forgiveness you've heard? A spouse forgiving a betraying mate? A parent forgiving a wandering child? A grieving family forgiving a drunk driver?
- How does the knowledge that God forgives and removes our past sins give us peace to go forward?

Apply:

Perhaps no act of kindness is so precious as the granting of forgiveness. The English poet Alexander Pope said that "to forgive is divine." And indeed, it takes the life of the divine in us to forgive another. We cannot manage it on our own. Without the living, enabling power of the Holy Spirit at work in our hearts, we are incapable of true forgiveness. But with Him, we can do all things.

We are able to forgive others because God, through Christ, forgave us. He knew our transgressions, He calculated the price we had to pay, He loved us too much to let us go, and He provided a way to write off the debt. It cost the blood of His Son. And because that death was immeasurably precious, there is no sin that He will not forgive if we bring it to Him.

When we practice forgiveness, we are truly reflecting the heart of our Father in heaven. Seeking His heart helps us realize how much we have been forgiven and how we can pass that on to others.

Pray:

Heavenly Father, thank You for forgiving me of my great debt of sin against You. Enable me through the power of the Holy Spirit to forgive those who wrong me. I ask in Jesus' name. Amen.

HIS EVERLASTING KINGDOM

Read Isaiah 9:6–7

Key Verse:

Of the increase of His government and
peace there will be no end, upon the throne
of David and over His kingdom, to order it
and establish it with judgment and justice
from that time forward, even forever.
The zeal of the Lord *of hosts will perform this.*
Isaiah 9:7 NKJV

Understand:

- What do you imagine when you hear the word *dynasty*?
- What is different between a human dynasty and the reign of Jesus as King of Kings and Lord of Lords for eternity?

Apply:

These verses from Isaiah are forever sealed in our minds as "Christmas" verses. And yes, they are tied to the promise of the Child that was to be born. But they are also eternity verses. They tell us of the permanence of the kingdom that is to come and remind us that we can trust the God who promises.

When we speak of earthly dynasties, it's usually in a negative sense. Royal families keep a tight grip on their kingdoms, and down through history, some were unwilling to relinquish that position. Their hold on power and fortune was more important to them than the welfare of the people under them.

Jesus is the King who died for His subjects. He is the royal who left His throne to become like the people He rules. He is the monarch who welcomes us into His family. The reign of Jesus will not be marked by policies that place Him out of our reach, but by righteousness and justice and fellowship with the one who already rules the kingdoms of our hearts.

Pray:

O God, I proclaim that You are sovereign in my life, and I look forward to the day when I can live in Your kingdom. Where You rule, there is peace and light and purity. Thank You, Lord. Amen.

ACKNOWLEDGING *EL ELYON*: GOD MOST HIGH

READ DANIEL 4:34–37

Key Verse:

Now I, Nebuchadnezzar, praise and extol and honor the King of heaven, for all his works are right and his ways are just; and those who walk in pride he is able to humble.
DANIEL 4:37 ESV

Understand:

- What is the difference between animals and people?
- What does the story of Nebuchadnezzar teach us about God's creation of man and about His oversight of the earth?

Apply:

Animals are gifts to us. God created them to reflect His majesty and creativity. He imagined their intricate ways and cunning habits; He gave them their instincts and beautiful coloring. Animals are His property, and we are never to treat them cruelly or neglectfully. We are to be stewards of His creation. Humane butchering and kind keeping of livestock are in harmony with God's Word, but flippant abuse is not.

In this story of Nebuchadnezzar that sounds like a retelling of "Beauty and the Beast," the proud king was humbled by the Almighty. His hair grew long like feathers, and his nails grew pointed like claws. He was driven out of the palace and lived in the fields. At the end of this lesson of learning, he accepted his rightful place in God's dominion and was restored to his throne. He was not meant to be an animal, but neither was he meant to be God.

One of the names of God is El Elyon. No one can take His place or usurp His authority. He alone rules heaven and earth. When we know our place and how to fill it, we are happiest. And He takes care of the rest.

Pray:

Thank You, God in heaven, for being almighty and sovereign. This world with its creatures and humans is Yours. Help me fill my rightful place in it for Your glory. Amen.

GOD, THE HELPER

READ PSALM 46:1–5

Key Verse:

> *God is our Refuge and Strength [mighty and impenetrable to temptation], a very present and well-proved help in trouble.*
>
> PSALM 46:1 AMPC

Understand:

- When did you last need help with something beyond your ability?
- Do you make a habit of calling out to God when you're in trouble? Why or why not?

Apply:

The key verse from today is familiar to many of us. We may have learned it as children. We know in our heads that calling on God is the right thing to do in any situation. But sometimes we don't do this, or we don't even think to do it!

This psalm from the Sons of Korah reminds us that even earth-tottering circumstances cannot shake the foundation we have in our God. There is no calamity or contingency that can topple His kingdom, and there is no storm where He is not strong and secure.

Often, we are not contending with big problems, but rather the small irritations and frustrations of life, with the everyday challenges in relationships and the temptations to please self instead of Him. In these circumstances too, He is the answer, the help that we need.

Today, refuse to go it alone! Turn to the one who promises help, in small or large amounts as we need it, and always when we need it.

Pray:

Father God, I need Your help today. I ask You to guide my words and my attitudes and to nudge me when I start to step out of Your will. Help me remember that You are my present help. Amen.

EL OLAM: ETERNAL GOD

Read Genesis 21:31–34

Key Verse:

Abraham planted a tamarisk tree in Beersheba and called there on the name of the Lord, the Eternal God.
Genesis 21:33 AMPC

Understand:

- What do you think about the tradition of planting trees to commemorate important events? Have you done this with your family?
- How does a tree symbolize longevity and solidity?

Apply:

Trees are an important part of the natural world. You can generally judge the type of region you're in by the trees and shrubs and plant life growing all around. The tree that Abraham planted was a tamarisk tree or a salt cedar. It likes moist soil but generally grows in the American West with blue-green foliage and small pinkish flowers; it can grow up to twenty-five feet tall. We're not told here why Abraham chose that particular tree, but we do know that it was important to him to make a statement about the covenant that he established there.

Families today often plant trees in celebration of a new baby or a career milestone or a specific relationship moment. Trees grow tall and last for years. They are a visual reminder that storms are not to topple us but to help us develop thick bark and deep roots.

God is eternal; He is more stable than the trees, but this visual helps us remember Him and His good work in us. As we seek to know His heart, we must remember that the Creator of the trees is the one who will stabilize us in the storms and prune us in the feasts. He is the eternal one—El Olam.

Pray:

Eternal God, my Father in heaven, thank You for standing constant. Thank You for working for good in my life. Thank You for giving us trees as a reminder of Your strength and eternal love. Amen.

THE HEALER OF EVERYTHING

READ MATTHEW 8:14–17

Key Verse:

And thus He fulfilled what was spoken by the prophet Isaiah, He Himself took [in order to carry away] our weaknesses and infirmities and bore away our diseases.
MATTHEW 8:17 AMPC

Understand:

- For whose healing have you recently prayed?
- Why is it important to understand that God is a healer as we seek His heart?

Apply:

Perhaps nothing is more requested in times of prayer than for healing for those who are sick and suffering. These requests are most likely more numerous than the petitions to save the lost! That isn't a good thing, but it does speak to the importance of bodily health. When we are sick and hurting, we cannot function well; many times, our spiritual health is affected as well. And all people, saints and sinners alike, must fight the battle with our fallen world and the effect it has on us.

One of the signs of the Messiah was that He would be a healer. Though Jesus fulfilled this, many missed the sign altogether or credited it to something else. How sad! Walking their dusty streets was the one who created them from the beginning, and they couldn't see it. They couldn't realize that He came to bring healing, not only of body and mind but of the soul. That is the ultimate healing.

One day, when we get to heaven, we will experience the amazement of perfect body, mind, and soul. And it's all because of Him, the healer of everything.

Pray:

Thank You, God, that You have the power to heal and to restore. Thank You for caring about our bodies as well as our souls. Today, I trust in the healing You bring, whether here or in heaven. In Jesus' name, amen.

EL ROI: THE GOD WHO SEES

READ GENESIS 16:9–15

Key Verses:

Then she called the name of the L*ORD who*
spoke to her, You-Are-the-God-Who-Sees;
for she said, "Have I also here seen
Him who sees me?" Therefore the well
was called Beer Lahai Roi; observe,
it is between Kadesh and Bered.
GENESIS 16:13–14 NKJV

Understand:

- Do you wear corrective lenses? Are you nearsighted or farsighted?
- Is the fact that God sees everything comforting or frightening to you?

Apply:

If you wear glasses or contacts, you probably remember your first pair of corrective lenses and what it felt like walking out of the optometrist's office with them on. Wow! The world was so clear and bright. All the blurriness was gone. All the indistinct edges. All the muddied colors run together. You felt like you could see everything!

God really does see everything—every tiny detail, every white lie, every dishonest action, every evil thought, every unkind word, every angry attitude. Nothing escapes His notice.

On the other side of that coin, He also sees everything that is good—every witness given, every helping hand offered, every gift of money to someone in need, every encouraging word for a fellow believer, every sacrifice for someone else. Nothing we do for Him is unrecorded in His book.

If you struggle with knowing that God sees everything, ask Him today to give you a new perspective. Then make up your mind to trust His heart and relax in His care.

Pray:

Lord God, the one who sees everything, examine my heart today and tell me if there is something I need to correct so that I can take care of it. Thank You for being a detailed God; I know I can trust You because of that. Amen.

IMMORTAL, IMAGINATIVE GOD

READ 1 TIMOTHY 1:12–17

Key Verse:

Now to the King eternal, immortal, invisible, to God who alone is wise, be honor and glory forever and ever. Amen.
1 TIMOTHY 1:17 NKJV

Understand:

- What does the word *immortal* bring up in your mind?
- How does the immortality of God produce reverence for Him in those who understand it?

Apply:

The word *immortality* has that classic, Victorian sound. It belongs in a big, fat dictionary with black-and-white lithograph illustrations. It's a word we might hear only at weddings or funerals or in the occasional hymn. But it has a powerful meaning. It means living forever, never dying.

Because our God will never die, He upholds all things forever. The universe is stable for as long as He wishes it to remain. The days on the calendar will keep rolling for as long as He ordains. The breath in our lungs and the beating of our hearts will continue until He tells them to cease. Nothing will keep Him from being the Lord of the universe.

At times, our days and weeks form monotonous ruts. And we somehow imagine that eternity will be like that—long stretches of endlessness, playing harps and looking at clouds. But immortality doesn't mean boredom. When we have the God of the ages to show us around heaven and to invent, from His creative genius, all kinds of wonders for us to explore, there will be no dull moments!

Toss aside your earthly ideas and anticipate what it will be like to get to heaven, the home of this immortal God who loves us and prepared a place for us.

Pray:

O God, I'm glad that You are never-dying. I'm glad that I know You and that someday I will live with You forever. Amen.

EL SHADDAI:
ALL-SUFFICIENT ONE

READ GENESIS 17:1–8

Key Verse:

"And I will establish My covenant
between Me and you and your
descendants after you in their generations,
for an everlasting covenant, to be God
to you and your descendants after you."
GENESIS 17:7 NKJV

Understand:

- What need do you have today that you include in your prayers?
- What is the difference between God's sufficiency and His will?

Apply:

There are times in our lives that are needier than others.

But yet, not everything we *feel* that we need does God supply. Sometimes it is His will not to fill the need or pay the bill or protect from harm. There are times when, for His own purposes, He chooses to take us through the fire and the flood and the storm. In those moments, He is no less El Shaddai than before. Instead, He is showing us that He can supply sufficient grace to help us bear the hardship.

God established a covenant with Abraham in which all the nations of the world would be blessed—from Abraham's descendants came the Messiah, Jesus Christ. God was sufficient enough to provide for this covenant through all the wanderings and prophecies and captivities of the Old Testament and into the New Testament era when a humble Jewish woman was found with child by the power of the Holy Spirit. And El Shaddai became a tiny infant and loved the world from a rough manger and then a rugged cross and finally an empty tomb. He was and is sufficient. And He will be that for us every day of our lives.

Pray:

O God who provides, I bring to You my requests and my needs. Fill them as You see best, and help me accept what You choose for me. In Jesus' name, amen.

UNCONQUERABLE GOD

READ JOB 42:1–6

Key Verse:

"I know that you can do all things, and that no purpose of yours can be thwarted."
JOB 42:2 ESV

Understand:

- Do you cheer on a specific team or political party or other organization?
- How does the victory of that group affect your sense of accomplishment personally? Why?

Apply:

We identify with those we cheer. It's human nature to attach ourselves strongly to entities we believe in and to feel as though we rise and fall with them. Some of us are more loyal than others. Some simply want to be on the winning side; they can't stand losing. Others will believe in their team's abilities and prospects in the very face of disaster.

But, in the context of our God, we need never choose between disloyalty and team spirit.

He will always win, and He always deserves our trust and devotion!

After Job was tested by Satan and then realized the huge gap in his personal understanding about the ways and workings of God, he confessed that no purpose of God could be conquered.

This is the confidence we can have in Him. We know that He can do all things and that whatever He chooses to do will be the best for all concerned. And if He wants something to happen, there is no one on earth or in the heavens who will keep it from being accomplished.

Pray:

God of heaven and earth, I delight in the fact that no one can conquer You and no one can stop Your ultimate purpose for me and for this world. I trust in You today. Amen.

ELOHIM: THE CREATOR

READ PSALM 100

Key Verse:

Know that the LORD, *he is God! It is he who made us, and we are his; we are his people, and the sheep of his pasture.*
PSALM 100:3 ESV

Understand:

- Why is accepting biblical creation crucial in our relationship with God?
- Do you think it's human pride that prompts people to repudiate creation and promote evolution? Why or why not?

Apply:

In the beginning, there was God and nothing else.

Everything we know came from Him. He put the particles on this planet for everything we now enjoy. He designed every facet of human life and family and relationship. He created all the atoms and molecules and cells that make up everything we see and touch and experience. Without Him, there is no earth; there are no animals or people. Without Him, there is nothing.

One of the greatest insults to a creative person is to attribute that person's work to someone else. In our terms, we call that plagiarism. Yet, people commit the most egregious plagiarism possible when they celebrate the idea that humans merely evolved from a lower form of life. When godless philosophers and scientists and professors credit some unknown force with the first speck of life that everything else flowed from, they are subtracting glory from God. When they say that it was all mere chance, they are robbing Him of the honor He is due. They don't want to admit that there might be someone bigger than they imagined to whom they might be accountable.

The Lord is Elohim—Creator. *He* made us, not we ourselves. He has made an investment in us because He crafted us for Himself and His glory.

Pray:

Thank You, Elohim, for making this world and everything in it. Thank You for loving us and sending Jesus to help us know You. You fill all and are above all. I love You, Lord. Amen.

TRIED AND TRUE AND TRUSTWORTHY

READ PSALM 84:10–12

Key Verse:

For the LORD God is a sun and shield; the LORD bestows favor and honor. No good thing does he withhold from those who walk uprightly.
PSALM 84:11 ESV

Understand:

- Do you trust people that you don't know?
- How do God's works demonstrate His trustworthiness?

Apply:

Trust is a golden gift. If there are people who trust you, you are blessed. You have probably earned that trust. Getting to the place where you totally trust another person takes time and experience. Unless they're family, we don't usually put total trust in another human being. And that's why God wants us to care for one another, depend on one another, and be true to one another in

His family, the church, so that we will be able to trust one another.

We are to follow in the example He sets before us. The scriptures reveal a God who always keeps His promises and who brings to pass what He predicts. The Bible tells us the stories of Jesus, who never failed His followers and whose word was true and sure.

Because we read the historical record of the Bible, because we know others who testify of His trustworthiness, and because we have experienced for ourselves that He can be relied on, we can happily concur with the psalmist when he joyfully states, "The LORD bestows favor and honor."

He will not keep from us any good thing that He deems is best to give us. Like a wise parent, He will always be looking ahead for us and guiding His hand of blessing toward that day.

Pray:

Dear Lord, thank You for proving Yourself trustworthy in my life. Thank You for coming through and for the stories in the Bible that help me remember it is true. Help me trust You more. Amen.

UNCHANGING LORD

Read Hebrews 13:1–8

Key Verse:

Jesus Christ is the same yesterday
and today and forever.
Hebrews 13:8 ESV

Understand:

- What kind of change do you enjoy?
- What is the most important point to you in the truth that Jesus never changes?

Apply:

There are at least two ways to look at change: positive and negative.

A positive approach could be that the change is an "update"—it is making things better than they were before; it increases the value.

A negative approach could be that the change is a "decline"—it is a signal that the previous status or condition has worsened; it is not optimal.

Neither one of these applies to our God. He cannot be made better. He is perfect in every way, holy and wonderful, and could not be improved. And He can never exist in decline, because there is no variation in Him and His holiness is never eroded. He is constant.

Many things in our lives will change this week, this month, this year. But He will not. When trials come, He will not change. When fortune rises, He will not change. When public opinion sways, He will not change. When death arrives, He will not change. When blessings accumulate, He will not change. This is the promise of the entire Bible, and for good measure, the Holy Spirit inspired the writer of Hebrews to put it down plainly. Generations of Christians have built their lives and established their souls on it. He is ever the same.

Pray:

Lord Jesus, I am so glad that You are always the same. I rest my life and my eternity on that. Amen.

THE KING OF GLORY

READ PSALM 24:1–8

Key Verses:

Lift up your heads, O ye gates; and be ye lift up, ye everlasting doors; and the King of glory shall come in. Who is this King of glory? The LORD *strong and mighty, the* LORD *mighty in battle.*
PSALM 24:7–8 KJV

Understand:

- Does biblical prophecy scare you or intrigue you?
- What do you imagine the coming of Jesus to earth as King will be like?

Apply:

I think many of us as children and teens were a bit frightened about the coming of the Lord. There are some stern warnings about the state of the world in times to come, and added to that, there is always a bit of apprehension about the supernatural. Remember how angels who appeared to people in the Bible usually said right away, "Fear not!"?

But the thing we need to remember is that the coming of Jesus is the best thing that could happen! He, the God of all time and of redemption and of every good gift, will not come to make things worse but to make them better. We don't understand all the details and all the interpretations, what is figurative and what is literal; but really, the most important thing is that we know Him in a personal relationship. He will take care of the rest.

When He comes back, those everlasting doors will open and the gates to Jerusalem will swing wide to welcome the King of glory. The glory He will bring with Him will cover us too, and we will forever be with the Lord. It sounds like a wonderful moment, after all!

Pray:

Jesus, I know You will return when it is the perfect time, when the Father signals that it is time for the wedding feast. I look forward to seeing You face-to-face. Amen.

TRUSTING THE GOD OF HOPE

READ ROMANS 15:8–13

Key Verse:

Now may the God of hope fill you with all joy and peace in believing, that you may abound in hope by the power of the Holy Spirit.
ROMANS 15:13 NKJV

Understand:

- What hopes and dreams did you cherish as a teen girl?
- How can our hope in God give us power?

Apply:

We tend to use the word *hope* in place of the words *wish* or *dream*, at least in the context of our conversations. We "hope" for many things that we do not have.

But the language of the Bible uses the word *hope* differently; very often it refers to something that is as good as done—a concrete, not abstract, reality. If we adopt this point of reference, many passages in the Bible, including this one, will mean more to us.

We serve a God of hope—not a god of abstract fantasies or a god of wishful thinking or a god of earning or a god of "maybe you'll make it," but a God of hope. Hope means our settled foundation in Christ. We don't have to wish that He will come through for us; He already has.

This kind of establishing hope gives us power in the Holy Spirit. This blessed third person of the Trinity is our source of joy and strength to live day by day. And so it is fitting that He is also the agent of our power.

As you go through your day, Satan will be sure to tempt you to find strength elsewhere and even to doubt that God's grace will get you through; but keep believing in the God of hope, and you'll be amazed at the grace He will give.

Pray:

Father God, I'm depending on Your settled hope today to ground me as I fulfill my responsibilities and follow Your Spirit. I want to use the power You give me to bless others too. In Jesus' name, amen.

FOLLOWING THE GOOD SHEPHERD

READ JOHN 10:7–11

Key Verse:

"I am the good shepherd. The good shepherd gives His life for the sheep."
JOHN 10:11 NKJV

Understand:

- What do you know about sheep?
- Why, in the Bible, are people compared to sheep?

Apply:

Perhaps some of the most peaceful paintings depict a pastoral setting of muted green colors and a pasture of sheep. Rarely though do you see a shepherd in the scene; but he must be there, just out of sight, keeping watch on the flock, guarding them from straying, and planning for their next meal.

This is the picture that Jesus gives to us with His words in John. He is the good shepherd. There is no one who loves the sheep more or who is willing to sacrifice greater than He. There are times when we can't figure out where He is in the picture, but He is always there nonetheless. He is looking out for us and overseeing our care without fail.

Sheep are animals that must be led, and in Bible times they were often led by the shepherd's voice. He spoke to them, and they knew whom to follow, even with other voices around. Sheep tend to stray, but they are social animals and become stressed when they are isolated from their flock. They do best when in the care of the shepherd, and so do we.

If you want to get close to the heart of God, know that His heart is the heart of a shepherd who will never leave you.

Pray:

Father, thank You for being my shepherd. I place my trust in You and pledge to listen to Your voice as You lead me. Amen.

JEHOVAH JIREH: LORD WHO PROVIDES

Read Genesis 22:8–14

Key Verse:

And Abraham called the name of
the place, The-Lord-Will-Provide;
as it is said to this day, "In the Mount
of the Lord it shall be provided."
Genesis 22:14 NKJV

Understand:

- How has your faith been tested recently?
- Are there symbolic altars in your life where you have given God your best?

Apply:

The story of Abraham and Isaac and the altar where God provided is convicting to all of us. What trust in God Abraham showed! What dedication to do whatever God asked! What cooperation from Isaac, from whom we see no resistance or anger! What a marvelous ending as God gives the lamb in a glorious foreshadowing of the sacrifice of Jesus, the Lamb of God, on the cross thousands of years later!

In our lives, we will be tested too. Not in the same way, of course, but we will bump up against moments when we will have to make choices. We cannot blithely say we love and serve God and never expect to have to stand by our words. Faith that never needs to choose its priorities is not strong. God does not test us to torment us but to reveal to us where we are stubbornly clinging to our own way instead of His.

Our God, Jehovah Jireh, asks us to cast our full confidence in Him. Then watch as He leads and provides.

Pray:

Lord God, You are my provider. Thank You for supplying salvation and sanctification and all that I need to follow You. Let my life reflect Your praise. In Jesus' name, amen.

THE KEEPER AND SHADE

READ PSALM 121

Key Verses:

The LORD is your keeper; the LORD is your shade at your right hand. The sun shall not strike you by day, nor the moon by night.
PSALM 121:5–6 NKJV

Understand:

- What type of security do you have in your home?
- The Lord is our keeper, so why do bad things still happen?

Apply:

Security is a big business. People pay handsomely for security cameras and alarm systems to protect their homes and businesses and valuables. It's usually wise to do so, depending on where you live. Sound judgment and discernment are traits that go hand in hand with following Christ.

In a larger sense though, we do trust the Lord to watch out for us, to protect us while we sleep and while we travel, to keep away the dangers of life while we work for Him and care for our families. But we know, from living life in this fallen world, that Christians are not removed from any possibility of danger. We too are subject to the bad choices of others and to the laws of gravity and inertia and to the effects of fire and water and destruction.

So, what does it mean for the Lord to be our keeper?

He safeguards our souls, and He shelters us *in* His will. Though we can't readily understand why bad things are allowed to happen, we know that nothing can touch us except through Him. What He allows to happen, He will take us through. If He couldn't, then He would not be God.

And so, we can say with the psalmist that the Lord is our keeper and shade. We are always in His care.

Pray:

Heavenly Father, I rest my soul in Your care today and thank You for being my keeper. Amen.

JEHOVAH MEKODDISHKEM: GOD WHO SANCTIFIES

READ EXODUS 31:12–18

Key Verses:

And the LORD *spoke to Moses, saying,*
"Speak also to the children of Israel, saying:
'Surely My Sabbaths you shall keep, for it
is a sign between Me and you throughout
your generations, that you may know that
I am the LORD *who sanctifies you.'"*
EXODUS 31:12–13 NKJV

Understand:

- Which day in the week did the Lord God sanctify or "make holy"?
- What is the significance of our sanctification?

Apply:

To sanctify is to consecrate or set apart. God did this with the seventh day of creation—the Sabbath. He made it different. On that day, He rested. God, who doesn't need to sleep, rested. That is to say, He stopped working. Later, on Mount Sinai, He told Moses that one day in seven belonged to Him. When Jesus rose from the dead on the first day of the week, the early church began keeping Sunday as their Sabbath.

When it comes to people, God wants us to be set apart for His purposes as well. He wants to consecrate us to His service and to purify us for holy use. He wants to indwell us by the person of the Holy Spirit and to conform us every day into the image of Christ. As we surrender ourselves fully to Him, He will begin His setting-apart work in us.

Pray:

Holy Father, I want to be set apart for Your use and sanctified for service. Please accept the surrender of my life and future and use me as You will. In Jesus' name. Amen.

HE IS THE LION OF THE TRIBE OF JUDAH

READ REVELATION 5:1–5

Key Verse:

But one of the elders said to me,
"Do not weep. Behold, the Lion of the tribe of Judah, the Root of David, has prevailed to open the scroll and to loose its seven seals."
REVELATION 5:5 NKJV

Understand:

- Have you read the Chronicles of Narnia?
- If so, what was your favorite characteristic of Aslan? If not, what do you remember hearing about the books?

Apply:

Lions always capture the attention. They are too big and too hairy and too noisy to ignore! They are not called the king of the jungle for nothing.

As we think about Christ's name, "the Lion of the tribe of Judah," we have to ponder all that is wrapped up in it.

Lions are kingly. Lions are fierce. Lions are masterful. Lions are conquerors.

Some people imagine that the Lord Jesus is a mild-mannered, unassuming prophet, but they are wrong. Jesus is a humble servant of God and an obedient Son, the Bible tells us. But He is also the strong defender of righteousness and the King of heaven and earth. He will win the final battle over the devil, and He will be crowned in honor and victory and glory.

In today's scripture reading, the elders were looking for someone who could open the scroll. And the kingly Lion prevailed! As His followers, we can be assured that our King will fight for us and that He will win. Jesus is Lord of all.

Pray:

O Lord God, I submit to Your authority and I take courage in the fact of Your kingly authority. Today, I pledge to serve You with all of my heart. Amen.

MAJESTIC GLORY

READ 2 PETER 1:16–19

Key Verses:

We were not following a cleverly written-up story when we told you about the power and coming of our Lord Jesus Christ—we actually saw his majesty with our own eyes. He received honour and glory from God the Father himself when that voice said to him, out of the sublime glory of Heaven, "This is my beloved Son, in whom I am well pleased."
2 PETER 1:16–17 PHILLIPS

Understand:

- Have you ever seen an unattractive bride?
- What is it that makes all brides beautiful, even if on other days they might be thought rather plain?

Apply:

Eyewitness accounts are powerful. What someone actually saw and heard and experienced is often the thing on which lawsuits are won or lost. The impact of saying "I saw it" or "I heard it" is difficult to dispute. You are asking the person to doubt their own senses.

The apostle Peter gave us his remembrance of the moment when Jesus was transfigured before them—when God the Father allowed the disciples with Jesus to experience just a fraction of His heavenly glory. And they never got away from it.

As a bride in a wedding dress is transfigured by the glory of something that is above everyday life, so Jesus has a majesty that is not of earth. He left that radiance behind when He became a tiny infant and was born to a virgin peasant girl. But that glory is still His. And someday, we will experience it for ourselves. What a day that will be!

Pray:

Lord Jesus, thank You for leaving the splendor of heaven to be my Savior. I know that only when I see heaven and the royal majesty that is Yours will I truly realize how You humbled Yourself out of love for me. Amen.

JEHOVAH NISSI: LORD MY BANNER

READ EXODUS 17:8–16

Key Verses:

And Moses built an altar and called the name of it, The LORD Is My Banner, saying, "A hand upon the throne of the LORD! The LORD will have war with Amalek from generation to generation."
EXODUS 17:15–16 ESV

Understand:

- What is the importance of Moses' hands being lifted for the battle to be won?
- In what areas of your life do you need a godly friend to lift up your hands?

Apply:

The little Sunday school chorus says "His banner over me is love" in words taken from the Song of Solomon. Here in this context, the word *banner* is used to convey the victorious wave of triumph that God gave the Israelites against their enemies.

A banner is something to be displayed and billowed about and celebrated. A banner means something significant has happened or someone significant is present. Just think of the cavalcades of royalty and the stages set for important personages; there are usually banners or flags of varying sizes. Banners indicate importance and position.

God was a banner of victory for the Hebrews, and He will be for us as well. When we learn to let Him fight our battles, we can be assured of triumph. He will meet our enemy, Satan, with all the power of the Word of God and with the already won conquest over death and sin at the cross.

Pray:

God of victory, be my banner today as I go out into the world and do my best to honor You with my life and words. Stand in the gap for me when I am tempted, and give me Your wisdom in every situation. In Jesus' name, amen.

THE GUARDIAN

Read 2 Thessalonians 3:1–5

Key Verse:

The Lord is faithful. He will establish you and guard you against the evil one.
2 Thessalonians 3:3 ESV

Understand:

- When are you the most vulnerable to temptation to sin?
- What does the guardianship of the Lord mean to you in your daily life?

Apply:

One of the beautiful things about the great work *The Pilgrim's Progress* by John Bunyan is the way he illustrated the Christian life. Instead of thinking about abstract concepts, Christians could visualize discouragement as the Slough of Despond and were motivated to resist being held captive in Doubting Castle, where faith was the key to unlock the dungeon door. There are many other settings in the story that give the thoughtful reader a point of reference in their Christian journey—from the sinful city of Vanity Fair to the Valley of Peace where the Shining Ones waited to escort weary pilgrims to the Celestial City. As humans who are captured by images, we grasp on to these ideas and know that we must fight our battles as though against flesh and blood foes.

The apostle Paul wrote in 2 Corinthians 11:14 that Satan can appear to us as an "angel of light" with great deception as he tries to destroy us. In times like these, we may not even be aware at first that we need to be guarded.

But our God is a shield on every side for us. If we are walking with Him in the light and listening to His voice, He will guard us. He will not let us be taken down by our souls' enemy. Instead, He will ground us and guard us from the evil one.

Pray:

O Lord, I need You daily guarding against the wiles of the devil that come against me. I trust You to give me wisdom so that I will not be deceived. In Jesus' name, amen.

JEHOVAH RAAH: THE LORD IS MY SHEPHERD

READ PSALM 23

Key Verse:

Surely goodness and mercy shall follow me
all the days of my life: and I will dwell
in the house of the LORD *for ever.*
PSALM 23:6 KJV

Understand:

- In this most memorized psalm of all, what is your favorite phrase? Why?
- How does the concept of goodness and mercy tumbling behind you give you joy today?

Apply:

There is probably no other psalm more often committed to memory than this one. It is quoted by children and the elderly, recited at baby dedications and funerals, whispered by the dying, murmured by the grieving, and cherished by the masses. Its message is timeless and its origin is divine. These are God's very words, communicated to a human vessel, and preserved for us through the generations.

We already talked about God being our shepherd and what that means. This psalm adds other bits of detail and information. And it includes a coda and a cadence to wrap up the life that is lived in communion with the good shepherd.

Goodness and mercy—these delightful, indomitable twins—will never let us out of their sight as we follow the shepherd and listen to His voice. There can be no other outcome. To follow the shepherd is to experience His goodness and mercy. He will lead us home, one step and one pasture at a time.

Pray:

Thank You, Father, for being a shepherd, the good shepherd. I commit once again to Your fold and Your voice. I am so thankful for Your leading in my life. In Jesus' name, I praise You. Amen.

THE SHELTERING GOD

Read Psalm 61

Key Verses:

For thou hast been a shelter for me,
and a strong tower from the enemy.
I will abide in thy tabernacle for ever:
I will trust in the covert of thy wings. Selah.
Psalm 61:3–4 KJV

Understand:

- What kind of shelter do you need today?
- Are you prepared to make the choice required of you to benefit from the shelter?

Apply:

We typically think of shelters as places of refuge from storms. In certain areas of the country, there are strong funnel winds that become twisters or tornadoes. A storm cellar is a comforting place to ride out the monster. A harbor can be a shelter from a storm at sea, where ships and vessels of all sizes are in danger of capsizing from the fierce wind and waves.

The psalmist David asked the Lord to be his

personal shelter, to keep him up and away from his enemy. And let's not forget that David had real, live enemies. This wasn't mere hyperbole. It was a life-and-death kind of thing. He wrote about protecting the king's life and abiding before God forever.

While we might not have actual enemies in pursuit of us outside our back door, we can echo the cry of David when he asked for shelter. There are many emotional and spiritual enemies that we need a place of refuge from and many situations that we need a hiding place from the blast. The God we serve is just as able to be that for us today as He was for David back then.

Pray:

Thank You, O God, that You are a shelter and refuge. I bring to You today the fears I carry and the burdens that weigh me down. I ask for emotional and spiritual respite from the heaviness I've been carrying. Show me what to do. And let me rest in Your love today. In Jesus' name, amen.

JEHOVAH RAPHA: LORD WHO HEALS

Read Exodus 15:22–27

Key Verse:

"If you diligently heed the voice of the Lord
your God and do what is right in His sight,
give ear to His commandments and keep all
His statutes, I will put none of the diseases on
you which I have brought on the Egyptians.
For I am the Lord *who heals you."*
Exodus 15:26 NKJV

Understand:

- What health conditions are bothering you today?
- How have you prayed in the past about these things or about the health needs of loved ones?

Apply:

God always heals His children, but it is also always on His timetable. Sometimes He heals on earth, but more often, He heals in eternity.

The second option is one that we don't like. It's the last resort, the answer we struggle to accept when everything else hasn't worked out. It feels like we're second-class children if we "only" get healed in heaven.

Pain and suffering are part of the package of living in this fallen world. We are not exempt. We have bodies and brains that are susceptible to disease and decay. And we must not think that we know better than the one who died for us and who is preparing eternity for us.

The people of Israel were saved from the results of the bitter water that day, but there were other times when their consequences were not removed. All we can know is that we have put our lives into the healer's hands, and He does with us as He sees best.

Pray:

Thank You, O God, the Lord who heals, for being in control of disease and death. While You don't remove all suffering here because of the curse, I know that it will not be part of my eternity. I praise You for that. Amen.

HEAVENLY TEACHER

READ PSALM 25:1–5

Key Verses:

Show me Your ways, O LORD; teach me Your paths. Lead me in Your truth and teach me, for You are the God of my salvation; on You I wait all the day.
PSALM 25:4–5 NKJV

Understand:

- Who was your favorite elementary schoolteacher? What grade did he or she teach?
- Do you ask the Lord to teach you new things from His Word? If no, why not?

Apply:

The heart of God yearns for us to know Him—not simply to know His name and to recognize Him as Creator and Master of the universe but to know Him as Savior and Father and friend. And, if our hearts are willing, we can grow closer to Him every day. By His Holy Spirit, He will teach us, step by step and principle by principle, how to follow Him more closely.

A heart that wants to learn is so important for the child of God. A proud, resistant, stubborn heart thinks it knows best and doesn't want to be told what to do or to be made to realize that it needs to improve. But a humble, eager heart will intentionally submit to the authority of the Word and to the instruction of the Spirit. That Christian will grow quickly in the things of God.

A heart that resists will cut off its own energy supply, but a heart that opens up is a place where growth will happen naturally.

Knowing the heart of God means that we want Him to teach us, and we welcome His instruction and His discipline. Why don't you allow the Spirit to lead you up new paths and open your eyes to new truths?

Pray:

Heavenly Father, please teach me more about following You as I read Your Word. Open my understanding to deeper truth, and show me how I can surrender even more every day. In Jesus' name, amen.

A GOD OF GRACIOUSNESS

READ PSALM 145:1–9

Key Verses:

The LORD is gracious and full of compassion, slow to anger and great in mercy. The LORD is good to all, and His tender mercies are over all His works.
PSALM 145:8–9 NKJV

Understand:

- Do you know any woman whom you would title a "gracious woman"?
- What would you mean by that?
- In what ways could we say that the Lord is gracious?

Apply:

The Bible describes our God as being gracious—full of grace. He is also full of compassion, slow to anger, and great in mercy. What a beautiful picture! If we could be defined like that, how wonderful that would be!

Think of women you have known whom you would term gracious; they probably have some of these same characteristics. They are most likely kind and not easily provoked. Their self-restraint and disciplined attitude are beautifying marks.

Looking back through the Old Testament, it's surprising how often the Israelites turned their backs on their God and went into idolatry with pagan nations and how often they complained about the way their God was treating them. If God had not been long-suffering with their disobedience and whining, there most certainly would have been a different outcome.

We must be thankful that the God of the Bible keeps His word and has an unchanging and merciful nature. This does not mean that judgment will never come but that He does delay that day to give the evildoers a chance to ask His pardon and really live.

Pray:

Dear God, thank You for Your patience and Your mercy. You have given me second chances and beyond. When I stand in heaven someday, it will be because You were gracious to me. Thank You for loving me so much. Amen.

THE LORD OF HOSTS

READ PSALM 84:1–4

Key Verses:

How lovely is Your tabernacle, O LORD of hosts! My soul longs, yes, even faints for the courts of the LORD; my heart and my flesh cry out for the living God.
PSALM 84:1–2 NKJV

Understand:

- What is the most challenging aspect of regular quiet time with the Lord?
- The psalmist said he longs for the courts of the Lord. How can we increase our hunger to spend time with Him?

Apply:

The title "Lord of Hosts" has a military connotation. It could be rendered "Lord of Armies." Often in the psalms, the writers referred to the strength and might of the Lord, and this term continues that theme.

The writer longed for the meeting place with the Lord, and his very flesh yearned for communion with the living God. This can be our model for our time with our heavenly Father.

We need to learn how to yearn for Him and how to satisfy ourselves in Him. Perhaps we don't have the same desire because we really don't understand the value of who He is to us. The psalm writers often listed the attributes of the Lord and meditated on them in song and in word.

For example, this phrase "Lord of Hosts" or "Lord of Armies" could have special meaning for us if we are fighting an intense spiritual battle. It would resonate with us because of the circumstances in our lives. But we would not know this if we were not making a regular habit of Bible study. Why not commit to learning all you can about our amazing Lord so that the knowledge you gather can boost your faith when you really need it!

Pray:

Lord, I want to love You more and know You better. I ask that You would guide me because You see my honest desire to nourish myself in Your Word. In Jesus' name, amen.

THE LORD WHO IS ABLE

READ 2 TIMOTHY 1:8–12

Key Verse:

For this reason I also suffer these things; nevertheless I am not ashamed, for I know whom I have believed and am persuaded that He is able to keep what I have committed to Him until that Day.
2 TIMOTHY 1:12 NKJV

Understand:

- What requests are heavy on your heart as you begin this time with God?
- Satan wants to discourage you from spending time with your heavenly Father. How can you defeat his plan by bringing your needs to God in prayer?

Apply:

Many of us have heard it since we were young: Pray about everything. But often, though we know we should pray, we are tempted not to do it. Life is busy, the details are many, the requests seem like something we might fix on our own. . .and does God really care anyway?

But in the middle of all these thoughts is the truth that God is able. That's it. He is able. Sufficient. Prepared. Unworried. Unbothered. He is able for whatever you need today.

In times of discouragement, we forget the power of small things brought to Jesus—things like that little boy's lunch, which fed over five thousand, and that fish, which paid the tax debt for Jesus and Peter. These unimportant things were important, after all, to Him. Tell God your unimportant things today. He wants to hear them.

Pray:

Dear Lord, I come with my needs and my requests, my worries and my thanksgiving. You know what I need as I bring my list to You. Help me remember that You are able. For whatever I need. Amen.

AWESOME AND AMAZING, ALL THE TIME

READ NEHEMIAH 1:1–6

Key Verses:

And I said, "O LORD God of heaven,
the great and awesome God who keeps
covenant and steadfast love with those
who love him and keep his commandments,
let your ear be attentive and your eyes open,
to hear the prayer of your servant."
NEHEMIAH 1:5–6 ESV

Understand:

- When you think of the word *awesome*, what synonyms come to your mind?
- If you could substitute one of those words for God, which would be most fitting and why?

Apply:

Despite the travel that man has done to the ocean depths and mountain peaks and even into outer space, we have touched only a tiny portion of the awesome power of our God. The world He created is one of grandeur even in its fallen and decaying state. How much more beautiful will that bright land be when we are together with Him!

The word *awesome* does describe the "otherness" that we observe when we really think about who He is. In the scripture today, the prophet Nehemiah was crying out to God for help when he heard of the destruction that had taken place in his hometown. As naturally as breathing, he used the word *awesome* in his description of the wonder of God's person. Surely for someone so incredible, the tiny problem Nehemiah was having would be very easily fixed.

Actually, it wasn't such a tiny problem, since repairing the walls of Jerusalem was a massive undertaking. But, as Nehemiah knew, for our God this task was not too much; and as he described his God even to himself, it bolstered his faith.

Don't be afraid to mention the attributes of God when you pray, even when you're alone. It really does help your confidence in who He is!

Pray:

Lord, thank You for being an awesome and amazing God whose power is unlimited. I encourage myself in You today. Amen.

JEHOVAH SHAMMAH: LORD IS THERE

READ PSALM 73:23–28

Key Verses:

Nevertheless, I am continually with you; you hold my right hand. You guide me with your counsel, and afterward you will receive me to glory.
PSALM 73:23–24 ESV

Understand:

- Have you heard of the "comfort of presence"?
- In what ways can you be present for others you know who need a friend or who are hurting?

Apply:

How can you adequately describe the gift of a friend's presence?

To know that someone is with you in your moment, in your need, in your pain—there is nothing like it. It is perhaps one of the least practiced but most powerful forms of comfort. Another human being in the room, in the space, letting you know you're not alone and simply being on standby in case something is needed. . . It's beautiful.

The Bible tells us in these verses that our God is "there." John 1:14 (ESV) says that "the Word became flesh" (Jesus' earthly incarnation for thirty-three years), and when Jesus returned to the Father, He told us that the comforter, the Holy Spirit, would dwell in us.

God dwells in eternal and holy relationship—Father, Son, and Spirit—forever united in being and purpose and essence. And He made us relationship beings. He knows that we need to know that He is with us, just like that friend in the room.

How wonderful are the many promises in the Bible that speak of God's presence with us. Why don't you make it a habit to jot down the reference every time you find one and keep a list to encourage yourself when you feel alone?

Pray:

Thank You, Lord, for being a God of presence. Help me serve others by being with them as I am able. I love You. Amen.

INFINITE CARETAKER OF THE STARS

READ PSALM 147:1–6

Key Verses:

He counts the number of the stars; He calls them all by name. Great is our Lord, and mighty in power; His understanding is infinite.
PSALM 147:4–5 NKJV

Understand:

- Do you enjoy stargazing? Do you name the constellations?
- Take a moment to think about the number of stars and galaxies beyond what we can see, and then be thankful that we have an infinite God who takes care of them all.

Apply:

One starry night, the Lord God told His servant Abraham to look up into the heavens and that his descendants would be more numerous than the starry hosts. At that time there were no Hubble telescopes and no modern technology to take pictures of the expanse of space. But Abraham knew, even without all the machinery, that God was promising him a lot of descendants.

Stars have long played into our dreams and imaginations. The Bible tells us that God made the lesser lights for the night sky. And this psalm tells us that He has given a name to every one of them. Imagine that. . .except we can't. Our brains break down as we contemplate the time involved in saying each name only once, let alone keeping track of them every day! This is the infinite God who calls us to get to know Him better. Is it any wonder that we can trust Him?

Pray:

Father in heaven, thank You for the stars. Thank You for being God and for being in control. Because You know the stars' names, I know that You know mine. Let me reflect Your beauty today. Amen.

JEHOVAH TSIDKENU: LORD OUR RIGHTEOUSNESS

Read Jeremiah 23:1–6

Key Verse:

"Behold, the days are coming," says the Lord, "that I will raise to David a Branch of righteousness; a King shall reign and prosper, and execute judgment and righteousness in the earth."
Jeremiah 23:5 NKJV

Understand:

- What does the word *righteousness* mean to you?
- As a Christian woman, how can you promote righteousness in your daily sphere?

Apply:

The word *righteousness* is common in biblical language, but it's not one that we hear a lot in everyday conversation. If it is used, it's probably in the context of theology or in the political arena where it might have clout in certain arguments.

The Lord our God, this almighty Father who we want to know better, is a righteous Lord.

Everything He does is right, and every thought He has toward us is right. His motives are right, and His execution is right. His will is perfect, and He is never late. He is a righteous King.

One day, Jesus will rule the world in righteousness! What will that be like? It will be incredible to have truth acknowledged and justice served, to know that the righteous Lord is guiding the decisions. Until then we must do our best to bring righteous decisions to the places where we live and work and worship.

Pray:

O Lord, You are right in all You do, and I'm so grateful for that. I can trust that You will always do the right thing, and You will give me grace to live righteously before You. Amen.

THE GOD WHO IS NEAR

READ PSALM 145:18–21

Key Verse:

The LORD is near to all who call upon Him, to all who call upon Him in truth.
PSALM 145:18 NKJV

Understand:

- When do you feel most alone?
- If God is near to us, do you think Satan works overtime to convince us that He doesn't care?

Apply:

One of the tactics of Satan is to isolate his prey and make them feel alone and vulnerable. If we look in the Bible, we see stories of how Satan used or tried to use aloneness against God's creation: David alone on a rooftop of the palace, Elijah alone in the cave in the wilderness, Jesus alone in the desert when He was fasting, and other similar situations. The fact is, not unlike fragile antelope on the African plains, we are easier to conquer when we are separated from our family or from the community of believers. Isolation and loneliness are the enemies of spiritual victory and vitality.

Satan not only wants to separate us physically from those who could support us, but he wants us to believe that even God in heaven is far away and doesn't care. Nothing could be further from the truth, but Satan is the father of lies. And he often blends in just enough truth that it seems believable.

What can we do?

We need to have our moorings in truth so that we recognize his tactics before he can succeed. We need to make every attempt to stay close to our spiritual network. And we need to call out in faith to the God who we know will never leave us alone.

Pray:

Thank You, Father God, that You are near, that You do not go on vacation from Your responsibilities or go on strike because You don't like the working conditions. No, You are ever faithful and ever near. I'm so glad to be Your child. Amen.

THE DEFENDER OF RIGHTEOUSNESS

READ ZECHARIAH 9:11–15

Key Verses:

Then the L*ORD* *will be seen over them,*
and His arrow will go forth like lightning.
The Lord G*OD* *will blow the trumpet,*
and go with whirlwinds from the south.
The L*ORD* *of hosts will defend them.*
ZECHARIAH 9:14–15 NKJV

Understand:

- What does the word *defender* mean to you?
- Knowing that God will be your defender, how does that reassure you as you look to the next season of your life?

Apply:

In the American court system, there are attorneys whose role is to be public defenders. For those who come before the court without a lawyer, a member of this group would agree to represent the client without charge. This lawyer will be diligent to ensure that a proper and legal defense is presented in the client's case so that the court's rule of "innocent until proven guilty" may be upheld.

In the Bible, we often see the Lord as the defender of those who are following Him. He comes to their rescue or He shields them from destruction or He vindicates them before their accusers. And He does this out of love for them. They cannot afford to pay Him back for what He has given on their behalf, but He does it because He loves them. The Bible tells us that the Lord defends the people of Israel, the fatherless and the widows, and those who trust in His name. He is a God whose strength is blessing to the ones who know Him. And we can trust His righteous judgment.

Pray:

Dear God, thank You for defending those within Your care. Thank You for caring for the destitute. Thank You that all Your judgments are righteous. Amen.

ROCK OF REFUGE

READ PSALM 18:1–6

Key Verse:

The LORD is my rock and my fortress
and my deliverer; my God, my strength,
in whom I will trust; my shield and the
horn of my salvation, my stronghold.
PSALM 18:2 NKJV

Understand:

- Rocks are anchors in our lives. Who have been earthly anchors for you?
- How can you be an anchor for someone else by remaining steady and faithful?

Apply:

If you know anything about temperament types, you know that much of how we act and process information and form relationships can be attributed to differences in our general makeup. Some of us are optimistic and some are pessimistic; some are bossy and some are quiet; some are motivated and some are not; some are talkative and some prefer to listen. All of these traits will have a bearing on how we live our lives and even on the way the Holy Spirit works in us to conform us more and more into the image of Christ.

The Bible often uses the imagery of rocks to denote something solid and stable, a reference point that will not move. When our God is called a rock, it's because He is the stability in all our lives. He is the point we can anchor ourselves to.

As you think about your own journey, can you identify the moments when all you had to cling to was Christ? In truth, He is the rock every moment in life, but when everything else is failing, we can see more clearly the strength that He is.

As you think about your relationships with others, note some ways that you can point them to the true foundation in life. A word from someone they trust will resonate and guide them.

Pray:

O Lord, my rock, I center myself in You and know that my foundation is sure. Let me be a light to illuminate Your strength for others. In Jesus' name, amen.

CHRIST THE COMMANDER

READ JOSHUA 5:13–15

Key Verse:

And he said, "No; but I am the commander of the army of the LORD*. Now I have come." And Joshua fell on his face to the earth and worshiped and said to him, "What does my lord say to his servant?"*

JOSHUA 5:14 ESV

Understand:

- What spiritual battles are you facing this week? List three of them.
- If Jesus were physically in the room with you, what would you tell Him about these battles? How would you ask Him to help you?

Apply:

Spiritual warfare is a reality for Christians everywhere. Though the forces of Satan come against us in different ways, unique to our personalities and backgrounds and circumstances and relationships, the battles will never cease until we step foot in heaven. Because we live on this earth where our enemy tempts and destroys, we are subject to times of temptation.

But the hope and confidence we have is in the same one who came to the Old Testament leader Joshua. Many scholars believe that this was the preincarnate Christ standing before Joshua as he prayed about the challenges facing the Hebrew people. Soon, they were to assault the walls of Jericho, but it would not be in the way that the adversaries expected! And that is how so often the Lord fights for us! When we bring our fears and strife to Him and let Him lead the way forward, He helps us win the battle in ways that bring Him glory and give us victory.

Pray:

Dear Lord, the knowledge that You will fight for me gives me confidence and strength! Today, I lay before You the evil opposition that I am facing, and I ask for wisdom and victory and stamina as I stand on Your Word. In Jesus' name, amen.

GREAT MYSTERY KEEPER

READ DANIEL 2:44–49

Key Verse:

The king answered and said to Daniel, "Truly, your God is God of gods and Lord of kings, and a revealer of mysteries, for you have been able to reveal this mystery."
DANIEL 2:47 ESV

Understand:

- Have you heard the term "mystery bag" in the context of understanding God's ways and workings?
- How do you deal with the unanswered questions in our spiritual lives—do you face them with doubt or with faith?

Apply:

Throughout the Old Testament and even into the New Testament, we see where God worked through dreams and visions. Think about the various times that God told someone something through a dream—Jacob, Joseph, Pharaoh, Nebuchadnezzar, Daniel, Joseph the carpenter, Peter, and on and on. Then think about the times that God gave someone interpretations of dreams. One of those is in today's scripture reading.

Though God can and sometimes still does work through dreams, it is not His main method of communication today, when we have the written Word of God available to us in many forms and since the Holy Spirit is now at work in the world in ways He was not before. God still speaks, but not as often in dreams.

However, we still have questions about what He is doing, and there are times when we wish someone could explain things. It's in these moments that we must choose to trust Him, the great concealer and revealer of mysteries. In His time and in His way, He will let us know what we need to know in order to do His will. In the meantime, we must trust, based on our faith in His character and His promises. He does all things well.

Pray:

Father God, I trust You today with the things I don't understand. I rely on You to give me what I need today, and I leave the rest in Your capable, eternal hands. Amen.

GOD, THE HIDING PLACE

READ PSALM 32:7–11

Key Verse:

> *You are a hiding place for me; You, Lord, preserve me from trouble, You surround me with songs and shouts of deliverance. Selah [pause, and calmly think of that]!*
>
> PSALM 32:7 AMPC

Understand:

- What does it mean to hide *in* the Lord as opposed to hiding *from* the Lord like Adam and Eve and Jonah?
- How has the Lord hidden you from trouble in the past?

Apply:

From the game of peekaboo with babies to the frolic of hide-and-seek with little children, the art of hiding and being found captures our imaginations whether we're young or old. Parents and grandparents and aunts and uncles love to see the delight on a little face when the child is "found." And children delight in being found.

But there are times in our adult lives when we

want to be hidden, when we need a place to hide out from trouble. This is not because we want to evade responsibility, but rather because we need a place to recoup our strength and rethink our path and regain our emotional and spiritual balance. Our God does not encourage us to give up and hide from Him or from life's demands, but He does offer us a hideaway, a cubbyhole, a sanctuary to be nourished and strengthened in before going back out and conquering in His name.

Moses, the prophet, experienced the phenomenon of being hidden in "a cleft of the rock" (Exodus 33:22 ESV) while God's glory passed by. In our lives as well, we can cry out to our Father to give us a place of spiritual retreat where we can be refreshed by His Spirit so that we can meet the trouble of the day in His name.

Pray:

O God, You are my hiding place, and today I run to You for refreshment in my soul so that I can meet the demands of my life and ministry. In Jesus' name, amen.

THE CHRIST, THE MESSIAH, THE LORD

Read John 1:35–51

Key Verses:

One of the two men who had heard what John said and had followed Jesus was Andrew, Simon Peter's brother. He went straight off and found his own brother, Simon, and told him, "We have found the Messiah!" (meaning, of course, Christ).

John 1:40–41 PHILLIPS

Understand:

- Do you remember the day you realized that Jesus was your Messiah, your Savior?
- How can you live today with renewed joy in that realization?

Apply:

The Jewish nation looked forward to the coming of the Messiah since it was foretold to Adam. Once the earthly line of His descendancy was promised in God's covenant with Abraham, Jewish girls longed to be the mother of the

Christ and Jewish boys looked forward to conquering alongside Him. The oppressed and repressed people of Israel yearned for vindication and victory, for freedom from foreign captivity, and for prosperity and bounty in their own land. They didn't realize that more than physical liberty, they needed the liberation of their souls. Jesus came to establish a heavenly kingdom that would far outweigh any earthly reign. He cared about the suffering they were enduring under their oppressors, but He knew that fighting for the upper hand in the present conflict would give them only a temporary freedom. He wanted to release them from Satan's eternal hold. And through the cross, He did.

Sadly, many of Jesus' day did not recognize Him as the one they'd been awaiting. Many had the reaction of Nathaniel, who doubted that anything good could come from unexpected places. But the words of Andrew and Philip acknowledged the truth that those who follow Christ know to be true. He is the Christ, the Messiah!

Pray:

Lord Jesus, You are the true Messiah of both the people of Israel and all those who put their faith in You. Today, I confess that You are Lord of Lords and Lord of my life. Amen.

MEDITATING ON THE MOST HIGH

READ PSALM 92:1–9

Key Verses:

It is good to give thanks to the LORD, and to sing praises to Your name, O Most High; to declare Your lovingkindness in the morning, and Your faithfulness every night.
PSALM 92:1–2 NKJV

Understand:

- What feelings of inferiority have you experienced this week?
- How can acknowledging that the Lord is the Most High help us have a proper understanding of ourselves and our worth?

Apply:

Self-esteem issues are the struggles of those who are blessed. Seriously. If people are fighting for survival—facing the dangers of natural elements and fending off starvation and searching for water to drink—how they view themselves is not the top priority. But, when our temporal needs are met, we have time to meditate on the deeper issues of life. This is not to say that these abstract issues are unimportant, but rather that we need to recognize the natural hierarchy of living and how that applies to our emotional and spiritual struggles.

The elements of worship and thankfulness can help us ward off these higher-level battles. Realizing the truth that God is supreme and holy and good and faithful and that He has made us and loves us and redeems us gives us a "place" to be and a center for our thinking. Then looking around and recognizing all the ways He is providing for us physically and spiritually will develop in us a heart of thankfulness and expectancy. It is difficult to be depressed *and* thankful. A proper view with a love for Him and His goodness gives us a better view of ourselves.

Pray:

O Father, I praise You today because You are high and holy and good. You love me and provide for me. I want to be who You made me to be, and right now I focus my thoughts not on my deficiencies but on Your sufficiency. In Jesus' name, amen.

THE SUFFERING MAN OF SORROWS

READ ISAIAH 53

Key Verse:

He is despised and rejected by men,
a Man of sorrows and acquainted
with grief. And we hid, as it were,
our faces from Him; He was despised,
and we did not esteem Him.
ISAIAH 53:3 NKJV

Understand:

- Why was Jesus called "a Man of sorrows" in this passage?
- How does the thought that He suffered strengthen you in your troubles today?

Apply:

This chapter is often read during Holy Week as we remember the suffering and death of our Lord. This beautiful prophetic passage pulls us into the passion and pathos of the crucifixion and helps us realize how very much Jesus endured for our salvation.

The descriptions of Jesus as the suffering

servant are overwhelming when one digs into them. He is a man "of sorrows" or acquainted with sorrows, not only (most importantly) in these hours of abuse and pain but throughout His earthly life as He experienced what we experience—the pain and difficulties of life—and as He witnessed and intervened in the desperate conditions of others. Being God, He knew all things, but as the incarnate Christ, He experienced them with us. And He was beaten and tortured for us, in our place. He was so disfigured from the ordeal that the Bible indicates that those nearby turned their faces from Him as from one who had that dreaded disease leprosy.

When we feel beaten down by life and burdened with pain, we can find solace in knowing that He also suffered and that He is standing with us. Indeed He has borne the worse of it for us.

Pray:

O Lord Jesus, thank You for suffering for me. My trials and pain are bearable because You are with me and because You have conquered the worst on the cross. I praise You for going through that for me. Amen.

JESUS, THE NAME ABOVE EVERY NAME

READ PHILIPPIANS 2:5–11

Key Verses:

That is why God has now lifted him so high, and has given him the name beyond all names, so that at the name of Jesus "every knee shall bow," whether in Heaven or earth or under the earth. And that is why, in the end, "every tongue shall confess" that Jesus Christ is the Lord, to the glory of God the Father.

PHILIPPIANS 2:9–11 PHILLIPS

Understand:

- What is the meaning of your first name?
- The name of Jesus is highly exalted by God; how do you honor His name in your daily life?

Apply:

While there are many who have been given the name Jesus down through history, there is only one whom God has highly exalted. Jesus, our Savior and coming King, has an honored name because He has done what the Father gave Him to do, because He has triumphed over sin and death, and because He is Lord of all.

Many on earth do not recognize or honor His name or His work. We hear the name of Jesus used in profanity by those who don't know Him. They do not use other names to express surprise or disgust, only His. And while they know there is something special about it, they do not have an awareness of why they need to cherish and reverence it.

The Bible tells us that someday every single person who has ever lived will understand who He is and will bow on their knees and acknowledge Him with their lips. But we don't have to wait; we can praise Him today with our words and with our lives.

Pray:

Jesus, You are highly exalted, and I praise Your name today. Let me always give honor to You and be a light to others so they can be part of those who honor You now before that great day. Amen.

THE REDEEMER WHO IS ALWAYS WORKING ON OUR BEHALF

READ JOB 19:23–27

Key Verse:

"For I know that my Redeemer lives,
and at the last he will stand upon the earth."
JOB 19:25 ESV

Understand:

- What does the name "Redeemer" mean to you?
- Jesus came to redeem more than our souls. What will you give to Him today?

Apply:

In the Old Testament story of Ruth, we read about the kinsman-redeemer, the one who could buy back what was lost. Boaz was that one, and he brought Ruth into a relationship of love and restoration. This symbolized what was to come in the redeeming death of Jesus for us. We are the beloved of God whom He was not willing to lose. He redeemed us to Himself by sending His Son to pay the price and buy us back from Satan.

As redeemed saints, we recognize that our souls now belong to Him and that we will live in eternity with Him, but we might often overlook the fact that He wants to continue His redemption in our lives. Indeed, He redeems not only our eternal destination and our hearts from sin but also experiences and situations and relationships. He can take what has happened to us and "buy it back" in ways that help us heal and move forward. What has happened may not *be* good, but He can rework it *for* or *toward* our overall good.

Whatever has been happening in your life does not need to be a waste of your time or suffering, it can be redeemed and part of the forward motion of your journey in Him.

Pray:

Dear Father God, today I bring to You the recent happenings of my life. There are things that seem irredeemable, but I know that with You even ashes can be made beautiful. I place these things in Your hands today and ask that You would work on my behalf. In Jesus' name, amen.

THE STRENGTH OF MY DAY

READ PSALM 28

Key Verses:

Blessed be the LORD! For he has heard the voice of my pleas for mercy. The LORD is my strength and my shield; in him my heart trusts, and I am helped; my heart exults, and with my song I give thanks to him.
PSALM 28:6–7 ESV

Understand:

- What songs have been a source of strength for you?
- How can singing turn our focus to trust and faith?

Apply:

Do you know someone who whistles throughout the day? Generally, these people are lighthearted and resilient; they greet the world with an optimistic view and a word of cheer. On the other hand, do you know someone who voices complaints and difficulties on a regular basis? These friends tend to view life through an anticipation of hardship. Most often, individual personality contributes to the lens that we see life through. But even so, there are choices we can make to help ourselves toward a more generous and sunnier outlook.

Over and over in the book of Psalms, we find the writers intentionally turning their gaze on the goodness of the Lord and on His help and strength. These men were very human and acquainted with all the usual challenges and woes, but they knew the secret: having a fixed gaze on the Lord, our strength.

Many times, God has used the words and melody of songs to uplift our hearts and refocus our spiritual vision. Maybe humming to yourself as you work around your home or listening to worship music in your workplace or vehicle would help you maintain a consistent focus on what is good and lovely and praiseworthy. Why not try it today?

Pray:

Lord God, thank You for being my strength and my song. Today, I choose to focus on You and Your power. I rest in Your goodness. Amen.

THE PROOF OF LOVE IS SACRIFICE

READ ROMANS 5:1–8

Key Verses:

For one will scarcely die for a righteous person—though perhaps for a good person one would dare even to die—but God shows his love for us in that while we were still sinners, Christ died for us.
ROMANS 5:7–8 ESV

Understand:

- How has God demonstrated His love to you throughout your life?
- Have you thanked Him today for the gift of salvation?

Apply:

Stories of sacrifice capture our imaginations and our hearts. There is nothing quite like hearing a retelling of how someone gave up something valued for someone else. This is the real definition of love—what we individually are willing to sacrifice for another—and the basis of love in our daily relationships. When we are willing to deny or deprive ourselves so that someone else can benefit, we are acting in love, and this is especially true in a situation where the other person is unappreciative or even antagonistic.

The Bible tells us that we can know for sure that God loves us because He was willing to send His own Son to die for us before we even valued what He was doing! When we were rebellious and without hope, He loved us and wanted to bring us back into relationship with Him. He was willing to pay the awful price of seeing His Son mocked and despised and tortured and killed. He valued us so much.

Whenever you are tempted to doubt the love of God for you and whenever Satan tells you that God has forgotten about you, look to the cross of Christ! Remember that love sacrifices, and be strengthened in the fact that you are loved beyond anything you can imagine.

Pray:

O God, thank You for loving me to such a depth! Thank You for sacrificing Your Son for me. Help me pass this love on to others, even when it requires sacrifice. I ask this in Jesus' name. Amen.

CHRIST, OUR VICTORY IN ALL THINGS

READ 1 CORINTHIANS 15:54–58

Key Verse:

> *But thanks be to God, who gives us the victory through our Lord Jesus Christ.*
> 1 CORINTHIANS 15:57 ESV

Understand:

- What spiritual victory do you need today?
- What are you willing to surrender to experience victory in Christ?

Apply:

The thought of victory enables us to surrender many things. Athletes surrender personal time to train; parents surrender convenience to mold; musicians surrender moments of leisure to practice; missionaries surrender comfort to evangelize. When we prioritize the accomplishment of a greater good, of a higher goal, we are willing to surrender our personal wants and, sometimes, even needs.

Jesus won the victory over sin and death

on Calvary's cross. This victory was total and complete. The battle does not have to be fought again. The Bible tells us that He has the keys to hell and death. He is the utter victor.

And because He has won the big battle, we know that there is nothing too difficult in our lives for Him to help us gain victory. There may be personal cost to us though, and this is where we prove our determination and commitment. If we are to be free of a besetting sin, we will have to surrender our desire for gratification, that pull to gain pleasure in a way that is outside God's boundaries for us. If we are to be free of doubt, we must surrender our inclination to look with cynicism at the world and look with grace instead. And on and on. As we relinquish our way of thinking and grasp hold of His, we can then be victors with Him in everyday things. This is the beauty of life with Christ. We have victory now and victory for eternity!

Pray:

Lord Jesus Christ, You are the victor! You have conquered everything for me, and all I need to do is tap into that victory by surrendering my way to Yours. By faith, I do that today. Amen.

THE ONE WHO IS WORTHY OF WORSHIP

READ REVELATION 5:9–14

Key Verse:

"Worthy is the Lamb who was slain,
to receive power and wealth and wisdom and
might and honor and glory and blessing!"
REVELATION 5:12 ESV

Understand:

- How does the worthiness of Christ impact your life today?
- What praise will you give Him as you join the saints on earth and the hosts of heaven in proclaiming His worth?

Apply:

The word *worship* comes from the Old English "worth-ship" meaning the ascribing of highest worth. Because something or someone is esteemed to be of highest value, worship is given. We can see a lesser form of worship in the context of earthly royalty. They are "worshipped"—or as we would say, respected or honored—because of their value, their position.

When we think of worship of our Lord, we recognize at once that there is nothing and no one higher or greater. He is the one above all, the King of Kings and Lord of Lords. We ascribe to Him the highest degree of honor. That is why we devote our lives and futures to Him and follow His words and align ourselves with His commands. We want to show our reverence for Him in daily worship—the outflow of our lives in our being, our words, and our actions. It's not a formal, boring existence, but a vibrant living out of everything good and beautiful in awareness that He is the center of all that we know and love.

Pray:

Father God, today I give my worship to You. Your worth is beyond anything else in my life. I want my life to be a beautiful outflow of worship in everything I do, and someday I want to worship You face-to-face as I live with You for eternity. In Jesus' name I pray these things. Amen.

ABOUT THE AUTHOR

Valorie Quesenberry is a minister's wife, mother, grandmother, musician, and author. She periodically contributes devotionals to a Christian literature provider. She has published with Wesleyan Publishing House and Barbour Publishing and writes both fiction and nonfiction.